Conflict Management

Jennifer Martin

Conflict Management

G
P

Dedicated to our children

Conflict Management
ISBN 978 1 76109 209 1
Copyright © Jennifer Martin 2022
Cover photo by Sunyu on Unsplash

First published 2007
This revised third edition published 2022

GINNINDERRA PRESS
PO Box 3461 Port Adelaide 5015
www.ginninderrapress.com.au

Contents

Introduction

In this third edition of *Conflict Management*, new content has been included on emotional literacy, self-care, the use of technology for e-mediation, conflict and criminal justice theories, an expansion of criminal justice as a field of practice including the concept of therapeutic jurisprudence, and a new chapter on international peace and security. As in the previous editions, management is used throughout as the preferred term to resolution in recognition of the centrality of conflict and change in everyday life. Conflict is a normal part of everyday life and dialogue is the key to effective conflict management. A range of factors influence how we view and treat others. Often, people are attracted to each other due to perceived similarities; they feel a connection or bond due to a shared interest or feature. In the same way, people can be rejected due to differences, particularly those not deemed socially desirable or valued.

There are things we do to be inclusive and accommodating of others, and to prevent conflict from developing, such as behaving in ways that are considerate and respectful. Usually this occurs naturally; however, in other instances, rules of engagement or codes of conduct are developed to promote what are considered to be proper behaviours in particular contexts. Self-regulation may take the form of a group managing members who transgress these rules. Or, for more serious breaches, law enforcement agencies may be asked to intervene. The penalty may be a warning, a fine or curtailment of liberties.

Increasingly, however, logical consequences are being used as a means of teaching people to behave responsibly. For instance, a man charged with breaching water restrictions during a drought had his water supply severely reduced by the local water authority. To teach him a lesson, the penalty was clearly related to the perceived misbehaviour, with the message loud and clear: 'You waste water – you go without.'

In civil matters where people have been unable to amicably resolve their differences, assistance is often sought from a third-party mediator. This may be a family member, friend, colleague, community or religious leader, or an independent mediator. What is essential in the choice of mediator is that all parties respect their ability to manage a fair and equitable process.

Over the past three decades, an industry in mediation and conflict management has developed. This is supported in legislation, policies and regulations that require disputing parties in certain jurisdictions, particularly when family disputes are involved, to attend mediation or another conciliatory conflict resolution process before being eligible for a court hearing. Often in other civil (and increasingly in criminal) jurisdictions, a matter is briefly heard in court and then referred to mediation. These more conciliatory approaches are seen to produce better outcomes at a reduced cost and are generally preferred by disputing parties.

As a social worker, I have practised mediation for over twenty years and am an accredited mediator. I have noticed a number of changes over the years, including the increased dominance of the professions, particularly lawyers, and different claims to expertise. It is an area of practice where, dare I say, there is considerable conflict in terms of professional jealousy, rivalry and claims of superior practice, both between and within the different professions. Some social workers claim that mediation is not a priority area of practice, as the mandate of social work is to work with the most disadvantaged and disenfranchised members of society, with mediation models not taking adequate account of social injustices. Planners are now required to undertake studies in mediation and conflict resolution, although some are not convinced of the need to do so.

There has been an increase in the number of trained mediators, without the anticipated increase in the demand for such services. It has been suggested that this lack of take-up of mediation services is due to public ignorance, or misconceptions of who mediators are and what they can do. The situation has now changed, as in many instances mediation is no longer voluntary but rather mandated by the courts. In many jurisdictions, conflicting parties are required to undergo mediation whether they want to or not. This has seen a marked growth in mediation services and training programs.

The challenge is to view conflict broadly and look at learning in conflict management and mediation as both a life and a vocational skill. The skills covered in this book are transferable to many different settings and can enhance opportunities for career change and advancement.

In chapter 1, on conflict and communication, conflict is explored as a normal everyday experience. A focus is on self-reflection and an understanding of the roles people play in conflict situations. This assists in conflict analysis and developing ways to manage it effectively. Personal and social factors that influence the way people communicate with each other are explored, including the impact of life experiences and personality type, expectations of others and an expanded section on emotions and emotional literacy. Fear and anxiety, shyness and self-blame are explored as barriers to effective communication. Principles for effective cross-cultural communication are presented, with an emphasis on respect for different cultural beliefs, values and ways of behaving.

Chapter 2 focuses on understanding conflict, in particular the significance of the conflict, the context in which it is occurring and the level, or stage, the conflict has reached. The main types of conflict resolution are explored, including litigation, arbitration, mediation, conciliation, negotiation and facilitation. Power is discussed as a central aspect of all conflict situations, with an analysis of power relationships essential for effective conflict management. The main behaviours in conflict situations – fight, flight and assertiveness – are examined, and skills in assertiveness and listening are presented as the keys to effective communication. How people are portrayed in conflict situations as aggressors, victims and rescuers is explored. The stress on workers in conflict management and mediation is acknowledged, and additional content and techniques are presented for mediator self-care.

Models, and approaches to mediation and conflict management, are discussed in chapter 3. Mediation models include settlement, facilitative, therapeutic, narrative, evaluative, preventive and policy-making. The more recent collaborative family law model is also presented. Approaches discussed are the win/win approach that aims to meet as many needs and concerns as possible of all parties, and the mutual gains approach that endeavours to maximise gains for all parties in the negotiation process. The similarities and differences of these models are considered and a model presented that encapsulates the core common processes. This model is divided into the two phases of problem-defining and problem-solving. Core talents and skills for mediators are identified, including process management and strategic intervention, investigation, presentation and discussion, inventiveness and empathy. Practice standards, codes of ethics, legislation and employer requirements are also considered. A new section has been added on the use of technology for e-mediation.

Main theories relevant to conflict prevention, management and resolution are presented in chapter 4. These include the social work critical theories: structural, feminist, anti-oppressive and anti-discriminatory, and postmodernism. The emphasis of these theories is on social justice, anti-discriminatory practices and power imbalances. Sources of possible discrimination and oppression considered are class, gender, race, ethnicity and culture, disability, age, sexuality and spirituality. Psychodynamic and life stage theories are also discussed, with these theories providing valuable insights into people's behaviours and needs at different times of their lives. This third edition includes additional information on negotiation theory and in particular game theory. A new section has been added on theories of particular relevance to mediation and conferencing in justice settings such as desistance, social learning, deprivation and importation. A model for integrating personal reflections, theory and practice – the Theory and Practice Spiral – is presented.

In chapter 5, the stages of problem-defining in the mediation process are examined. These include intake, to determine the appropriateness of mediation, and orientation. Private session is discussed, as well as the use of shuttle mediation in situations where it is not appropriate to have the parties in the same room together. The skills of empathy and probes are explored, with guidelines for developing empathic responses. The storytelling stage includes consideration of language, memories and emotions and how these impact upon a person's perceptions and recollection of events. Consciousness-raising and discourse analysis are useful for analysing stories in terms of power, positions, meanings, behaviours and values. Identification of main issues and agenda setting are discussed and how the skill of reframing assists in developing new shared perspectives and more positive ways of communicating.

Chapter 6 examines the stages in the problem-solving phase of the mediation process. Developing options and mapping the conflict looks at the interests, needs and concerns of each party and is particularly useful in complex multi-party disputes. Selecting options, negotiation and decision making includes consideration of the application of the principle of least contest and the mutual gains approach. This is followed by agreement preparation, implementation and follow-up.

Main areas of mediation and models of practice are presented in chapter 7, including parent–adolescent and family dispute resolution. Adult–elder mediation, a growing area of mediation practice, is explored and the skill of advocacy. A closer look is taken at dementia and associated mediation tasks. Workplace disputes also are considered. The section on dispute resolution processes used in the justice system, including family group conferencing and victim/offender mediation has been updated and expanded to include a new section on therapeutic jurisprudence. Neighbourhood and planning disputes are discussed and the role of the planner as conciliator.

Chapter 8 focuses on complex multi-party environmental conflicts. A model of policy-making mediation is presented as particularly suited to complex multiparty disputes that require the development and implementation of policies, standards, procedures and regulations. It is well suited to international conflicts including issues of economic development and environmental and social sustainability. A case study of policy-making mediation in the Mekong River Basin illustrates the application of policy-making mediation in an international context.

This edition includes a new chapter on international peace and security. Key aspects of violent conflicts are explored, including general techniques for the prevention of violence. Sources of conflict and key actors on both intra-state and interstate levels are examined. International conflict is analysed using the cyclical process to determine the level of the conflict and most appropriate responses for conflict prevention, containment and peacekeeping, transformation and reconciliation. This includes consideration of private military forces and the use of technology and artificial intelligence.

This book covers the substantive knowledge and skill development required for effective conflict management and mediation practice at beginning, intermediate and advanced levels. It is intended for people who plan to practise as mediators or perform other roles in conflict prevention, management and resolution. This includes all discipline areas that practise in mediation and conflict resolution: criminology, legal and justice, social work, psychology, youth work, planning and environment and international development. It is also relevant to other disciplines, as well as community mediators who may not be aligned with a particular discipline area.

The numerous exercises and questions throughout this book are intended to stimulate critical thinking and reflection. Scenarios and exercises are drawn from my own experiences as a social worker working in conflict management and mediation; all personal identifying information has been changed.

I hope that this book provides you with useful ideas and suggestions to stimulate and inform your thinking and practice and to embrace the challenges presented.

1

Conflict and Communication

Understanding ourselves and the roles we play in conflict situations is central to understanding conflict. Conflict arises primarily due to four main reasons:

1. competition for limited resources
2. principles at stake
3. territory
4. relationships.[1]

Conflict over resources generally evokes strong emotions. If these emotions are not addressed and managed appropriately, the conflict is not likely to be resolved. Successful conflict prevention, management and resolution requires skilful communication that addresses both content and emotion. Interactions with other people necessarily result in different ideas, views and opinions. Judgements are made and opinions formed on the basis of what is said and not said. An important consideration is purpose and context of the communication. The answers to the following three questions will assist in determining the most appropriate process and skills to use to manage a conflict situation:

1. What is the purpose of the interaction?
2. Is the type of communication that is occurring deemed appropriate to the particular circumstances and setting?
3. Is the communication voluntary or do these people need to communicate for a particular purpose?

Power is a central feature of all conflict situations. Power can be assumed or exercised for a number of reasons, including assumptions of superiority due to ability, age, class, gender, race, ethnicity and culture, sexuality and spirituality. An analysis and understanding of the exercise of power in relationships is essential for effective conflict management. The focus of this chapter is on developing a greater understanding of use of self in conflict situations and how different personality types and other factors influence the quality of interactions with others. Emotions are explored, as well as consideration of barriers to interpersonal effectiveness, particularly fear and anxiety. The role of culture and principles for effective cross-cultural communication are highlighted.

Communication in conflict situations

A number of factors affect interpersonal communication. The degree to which we understand ourselves, and how what we do and say impacts upon others, necessarily influences the communication process and outcomes. How often in situations of conflict have you said or heard others say, 'What did I do?' Sometimes people seem oblivious to having any part in what has occurred, preferring to find fault with and to blame the other person.

> A worker and three members of the local community were referred to mediation by the coordinator of a neighbourhood house. The coordinator described conflict between these four people that had resulted in members of the local community refusing to participate in activities at the house. As well, one member had threatened legal action due to defamatory comments made by the worker. I accepted this referral and proceeded to make contact with all of the four people who had been referred. In turn they told me that I had the wrong person and that they were not in need of mediation. The problems were personalised as belonging to particular individuals who simply needed a good talking to.

Communication is influenced by personality type. Someone who is more introverted will communicate very differently to a person with a more extrovert and outgoing personality. Often the former can mistakenly be seen as aloof or unfriendly and the latter brash and insensitive. The quality of your presence with others determines the effectiveness of the communication that occurs and influences how conflict situations are managed. Fear and anxiety can cause people to avoid communicating with others, and interactions that do occur seem awkward. In such situations, messages are often misinterpreted, as the communication is not free-flowing.

A general understanding of conflict is necessary, as well as a detailed knowledge of particular conflict situations, if the conflict is to be managed appropriately. Conflict management is often the primary objective. This is not to undermine conflict prevention and resolution processes. It is rather to acknowledge the centrality of conflict in our daily lives. Conflict is something to anticipate and respond to rather than avoid or resolve.

Many positive aspects to conflict are often overlooked. Conflict provides opportunities for change that need to be embraced rather than avoided.[2] This includes opportunities to develop deeper understandings of problems or situations from the views and perspectives of others. It also provides feedback on how others perceive you and your behaviours due to these increased understandings. Effective conflict resolution strategies strengthen relationships and provide a basis for further conflict management in the future. Third parties are sought in situations wherein people have not been able to communicate effectively and resolve their differences amicably.

Conflict management is a growing area of practice, with people increasingly being diverted from litigation (an adversarial way of resolving disputes) to other more conciliatory processes. The manner in which the conflict is managed by a third party can often determine whether or not further communications will occur. For instance, in a building dispute, a payout may occur rather than the builder having to rectify outstanding works.

Understanding ourselves in conflict situations

Self-reflection and self-awareness are necessary for effective communication. This requires an understanding of personal needs, weaknesses and strengths. Recognition of personality type and preferred style of communication, and acknowledgment of the impact of current and previous life experiences, will impact upon the conflict management process.

Life experience will also influence perceptions of others and their circumstances. Often, people are attracted to, and interact with, those with similar values and beliefs and lifestyles. Difference can provide challenges to personal values and beliefs as well as discomfort. Effective communication requires openness and the freedom to perceive with clarity and relate with honesty – regardless of how similar or different others may be. This includes an ability to perceive and evaluate values, attitudes and patterns of behaviour of the groups of which you consider yourself a part, as well as the ability to differ and stand alone when necessary. Sensitivity to personal patterns of thinking, feeling and behaviour that promote effective communication with others is required, as well as awareness of those that may interfere.

What groups do you belong to? Do members of these groups share similar values and beliefs to you? In what ways are members of these groups different from you?

Personality

Personality influences how we communicate with others. As mentioned earlier, a common way of distinguishing between personality types is the use of the terms 'introvert' and 'extrovert'. The problem with the dichotomy is that people generally do not fit comfortably into one of these categories. The ways people behave and interact with others is more complex and is influenced to a great extent by the context in which the communication is occurring. A further danger with these categories, or labels, is that they are all-embracing and the person's identity becomes associated with the classification applied. When having a personality profile done, a person may be told, 'You are an introvert.'

A more useful approach is to look at common qualities embodied in different personality types. Simply put, some people are quieter and others louder in different settings. Louder people are often seen as more confident and can be more at ease socially. However, quieter people can also be confident in ways that are perhaps less noticeable. Quieter people do not get the same attention and opportunities as those who are louder, and are often overlooked. A louder person may tell you of personal achievements while a quieter person may wait for you to notice.

When conflict arises, a louder person may be more likely to engage in behaviours that let the other person know they are not happy, while a quieter person's discomfort may not be expressed or noticed, particularly in the early stages of conflict. In later stages, it may be made noticeable by a stony silence.

Gill, the coordinator of a local consumer and carer support group, was in conflict with workers at a local hospital who saw her group as interfering with the work they were doing with their clients. The manager of the service requested a meeting to try and resolve this conflict. Gill consulted with me as to how to respond to this invitation. We discussed the possibility of her attending with a co-member of her support group rather than on her own, due to the imbalance in terms of numbers and power. Gill thought about this and decided to attend alone. Her reason was that other group members were louder and more outspoken than she was and she was concerned that they might dominate the conversation and she would not get an opportunity to speak because she was quieter than them.

Personality affects outlook on life, predominantly whether it is optimistic or pessimistic. This is typified by the argument over the glass half full or half empty. A person who is optimistic is generally more positive, whereas a person who tends to be pessimistic is more negative. This is reflected in expectations of self and others and is strongly influenced by past experiences. Outlook will also influence expectations of a third party conflict resolution process.

1. *How would you describe your personality to someone who has never*

met you before? Share this with a partner. Ask your partner for
feedback as to what their impressions are of your personality.
Is this how you see yourself?
2. *What is your outlook on life? Is it usually optimistic or pessimistic?*

Quality of your presence with others

The quality of your presence with others and effectiveness as a third party mediator is influenced by personal values, attitudes and beliefs. The level of conflict will influence this, as well as your ability to respond to issues, concerns and behaviours as they arise. Language is of crucial importance as it is the main medium used in interactions between individuals. This includes all forms of language, both spoken and unspoken. What is often referred to as 'active listening' involves

- observing and reading the person's non-verbal behaviour, posture, facial expression, movement, tone of voice;
- listening to and understanding the person's verbal messages; and
- checking for congruency between verbal and non-verbal communications.

Effective communication involves listening to and reading bodily behaviour, facial expressions and voice-related behaviour. This includes general appearance, physical characteristics and physiological responses. For instance, if a person is of a larger or stronger physique, do they use this to intimidate others? It is not uncommon for a person's face muscles to tighten and for them to become flushed when angry. This should not be confused with anxiety, embarrassment or guilt. It is useful to have a sense of the person's usual style of communicating in a more relaxed setting so that differences can be more accurately noted.

When listening to others, you are listening to them discussing perceptions of experiences, their own behaviours and those of others, their affect and points of view. You are also listening to what is not said but rather portrayed through non-verbal behaviour. Body language is very powerful and can be more relevant than what is being said. A person's body language can punctuate or modify interpersonal communication. This may be done by others confirming or repeating what has been said and by nodding in agreement.

A perplexed or puzzled look may suggest that the person is confused or is in disagreement with what has been said, or is perhaps processing new information. A person can use their body to add strength, or emphasise, what they are saying to appear more convincing. Checking for congruency between verbal and non-verbal behaviours is important. For instance, if a person is saying 'yes' and shaking their head 'no' at the same time, it is most likely that they disagree but are choosing not to say so. This is an indication that further discussion is required and the expression of agreement cannot be relied upon.

A person may also use non-verbal behaviours to control or regulate others. This may simply be a look, or it may be a signal or cue shared by the parties and not known to the mediator. The mediator needs to be attuned to such communications and respond appropriately so as to establish an environment and process that will foster open communication free from intimidation. Strategies and processes to assist are discussed in chapter 3 on mediation.

Due to family conflict and difficulties at school, Alex and her family were referred for mediation. Alex was sixteen years old and had an eating disorder that had resulted in several lengthy hospital admissions in the previous two years. Her schooling and social networks had been severely disrupted and the family was experiencing considerable distress. Several family meetings occurred with Alex and her parents and older sister and younger brother. Very little private information was shared by family members at these sessions. Each time a question was asked, the father would focus his gaze on the person the question was directed to. No family secrets were to be shared in his presence.

1. *What are you like when you are with and listening to others,*
   especially in a serious situation that may involve conflict? Think of
   a recent conflict situation and comment specifically on both verbal

and non-verbal behaviours, including tone of voice, posture and gestures, and facial expressions.

2. *What do you do well?*
3. *What aspects of your attending style would you like to further develop?*

People look for qualities in a third party mediator, including trust, respect and genuineness. They also have expectations that the third party mediator will manage a safe and effective process.

Complete the following statements:

1. *'If I was in a conflict situation that required the assistance of a third person to attempt to settle the dispute, I would like that person to possess the following qualities…'*
2. *'If I was in a conflict situation that required the assistance of a third person to attempt to settle the dispute, I would like the meeting conducted in the following manner…'*

Emotions

People generally speak through their actions, routines, daily work, habits and commitments to others. They do not usually speak about their thoughts and feelings, preferring them to remain private.[3] Level of expressed emotion is a choice made by a person and is influenced by a range of factors including social acceptability, gender, trust, context and culture. In making these and other choices, people determine how they see themselves and how they present themselves to others. For instance, a Western male may not feel it is socially acceptable to cry in public as it is likely to be seen as a sign of weakness. This is not to deny that the emotions are present.

Emotions are an important aspect of communication in conflict situations as they reflect personal experience of events. A mediator's own emotions, and relationships developed with the conflicting parties, are an integral part of the conflict management process. Workers in conflict situations are required to balance specific information about external events with internalised reflections on thoughts and feelings that are often not revealed.

Emotions and conflict

All conflict is emotional because it involves real and perceived threats to the achievement of individual or group goals.[4] Conflict transformation relies upon an understanding of emotional experiences yet too often in conflict management processes emotions are underestimated, misinterpreted or ignored.[5] In mediation, transformation of relationships may occur as a secondary process to the primary focus on reaching agreement on the issues in dispute. It has been argued that in conflicts where ongoing relationships are necessary, such as in workplace and family conflicts, that a focus on emotions and relationships, rather than interests, is more effective in terms of longevity of outcomes.[6]

Many and often conflicting emotions can be generated during conflict situations that may increase or reduce energy levels. Active negative emotions such as contempt, frustration, humiliation, hatred and anger generate negative energy characterised by activities such as gossiping and defamation aimed at socially excluding the other person or group. On the other hand, guilt, hurt, and sadness tend to reduce levels of arousal and inhibit ongoing interactions.[7] Webb cautions against categorising emotions as positive or negative as all emotions serve a purpose.[8] He identifies what he refers to as 'shame masking emotions' of distress, fear, anger and disgust. Zhang, Ting-Toomey and Oetzal distinguish between guilt and shame with guilt attached to actions and shame to the individual who is construed as a 'bad person'.[9] Halperin et al. differentiate between fear and hatred and argue that in deep-rooted political or sectarian conflicts, hatred is the greatest barrier to peaceful solutions due to the often long-standing belief that the other group is inherently evil.[10]

Ekman asserts that there are six universal emotions that are easily identified through facial recognition across all cultures.[11] These are happiness, sadness, fear, disgust, anger and surprise. However, others argue that emotions are sometimes misinterpreted, with Olson and Braithwaite[12] claiming that sadness, fear and disgust are often inappropriately identified simply as anger, and Zhang and others[13] finding that empathy is sometimes misinterpreted as compassion.

Conflict behaviours are generally categorised as collaborating, compromising, competing, accommodating or avoiding. These behaviours are used to pursue 'instrumental, relational and identity goals'.[14] Instrumental goals relate to scarce resources whereas relational goals are concerned with interactions and issues of trust, attachment and power dynamics. Identity goals are focused on the person's image or 'face'. Face is defined as a 'claimed sense of self-respect in interactive situations'.[15] Zhang, Ting-Toomey and Oetzal distinguish between 'self-face', 'other-face' and 'mutual-face'. Self-face is about protection and preservation while other-face shows concern for the other person's image. Mutual face is focused on the face of both parties and the relationship. Zhang, Ting-Toomey and Oetzal use conflict face negotiation theory to identify the complexities of culture and argue that all cultures have a high concern for face in communications. They assert, 'conflict is essentially a face-negotiation process, but cultural value orientations and individual attributes shape one's self/other face work and conflict behaviour'.[16] This results in people from collectivist cultures showing greater concern for other-face and mutual-face than those from more individualistic cultures who are more inclined to focus on self-face. This in turn impacts on the conflict behavioural styles, with more individualistic approaches leading to the adoption of competitive, dominating and aggressive behaviours. Those using a collectivist approach will more readily engage in collaborative approaches. In accordance with the theory of mutual gain, mediation relies upon collaborative behavioural styles and compassion.[17]

Conflict situations evoke physiological, psychological and social responses that are interrelated.[18] The following discussion groups relevant concepts under these three categories, noting that some concepts may fit under more than one category. Physiological responses to conflict are biological compared with psychological responses that focus more so on thought process and social responses that are concerned with behaviour and interactions.

Physiological

Conflict situations cause physiological and emotional responses, particularly as conflict levels increase. This is an unconscious process that informs cognitive appraisals and behavioural responses. Emotions are detectors of sensory stimuli that require a rapid response. Pessoa has developed a 'dual competition' model that forecasts increased executive control in response to emotional stimuli.[19] In accordance with this model, enhanced sensory perceptions prioritise information that is conveyed to control structures that allocate additional resources to respond. This model is supported by Kanske and Koz, who have found that the processing of conflict is sped up by emotional stimuli.[20] [21] Depending upon how this information is processed, this might result in fight or flight or assertive responses. Physical responses for fight and flight responses might include increased heart rate and breathing, dilated pupils, dryness of mouth and increased glucose release and adrenalin to boost energy.

A stress response will be influenced by the person's capacity to cope with the demands. Cortisol is produced in the adrenal cortex in response to stress levels with prolonged levels resulting in impaired memory.[22] Aloia and Solomon's study of physiological stress reactions to conflict within romantic relationships found a positive association between the intensity of the conflict and cortisol levels with affectionate and supportive communications lowering cortisol levels.[23] Higher rates of cortisol were recorded for those who had experienced childhood exposure to verbal aggression in their family of origin. They suggested that this childhood experience may serve as a coping mechanism reducing sensitivity and increasing ability to tolerate intense conflict. However, reduced physiological sensitivity may also result in the person not recognising early warning signs as well as an increased likelihood that they will also have higher levels of anxiety and possibly engage in aggressive behaviours.[24] Arbel, Rodriguez and Margolin's study findings also highlight the significance of family of origin experiences suggesting that this may also increase sensitivity to stress. They propose that the timing of when this past aggression occurred is worth considering as this may influence conflict responses in the present.[25]

A study by Mather and others found differences in cortisol levels between males and females when faced with the same stress inducing stimuli with males found to be more inclined to desensitise and women to sensitise.[26] Males with higher levels of testosterone demonstrated higher levels of desensitisation with no association found between oestrogen levels in women and stress responses. The claim that there is an association between high levels of testosterone and aggressive behaviours is not supported in a study of 998 men in Poland by Bloomer and others, who found that rather than having higher testosterone levels, aggressive males were more likely to be overweight and at risk of heart disease, diabetes and stroke.[27]

Psychological

Lazarus has developed an appraisal theory of emotions that incorporates a two stage cognitive process.[28] In stage 1, a triggering event is experienced, with the person assessing the situation according to goal relevance, goal congruence and ego involvement. In stage 2, the focus is on who is to blame, ability to deal with the problem and an evaluation of whether things are likely to get better or worse if no action is taken. Different emotions will be experienced during this appraisal process, such as anger if the conflict is assessed as unfair and related to identity and/or goal blocking. The adoption of cognitive approaches in mediation can lead to a reappraisal of the situation from different perspectives that may trigger a different response and emotion. This includes the person considering their own role in the escalation of the conflict.[29] This could be on an individual or group level. Group members are likely to experience group-based or inter-group emotions that will be informed by information provided by group leaders and other sources such as the media. Accordingly, this information has already been filtered and appraised by others who then decide on what the main messages and emotions conveyed are.

In the interactional approach to conflict management, Sillars has identified three subordinate strategies for dealing with conflict.[30] These are avoidant, distributive and integrative. In avoidant strategies the person keeps away from the other party and avoids discussion of the conflict. Distributive strategies are characterised by the person working against the other party. They may engage in explicit discussion that negatively evaluates the other party or attempts at compliance. Integrative strategies also use explicit discussion. However, evaluations of the other party are positive or neutral and compliance is not sought. Integrative strategies are considered most likely to result in positive relationships with avoidant and distributive approaches impacting negatively.

Emotional literacy is concerned with levels of awareness of self and others' emotions. 'Emotional literacy' is the preferred term in this text rather than the term 'emotional intelligence' as it more adequately reflects the concept using a strengths-based rather than a judgemental approach by someone taking a superior postion. A person may be more or less emotionally literate in a way that does not necessarily relate to their intelligence. However, most authors do use the term emotional intelligence and when this is the case, this term will be used. Mayer and Salovey have developed a sequential model of emotional intelligence that includes (1) perception, (2) assimilation, (3) understanding and (4) management.[31] Perception requires self-awareness and honest, accurate expression of emotions. Assimilation involves consideration of relevant information from various perspectives, including past experiences, before deciding what is important. Understanding includes the ability to understanding complex and conflicting emotions with 'management' concerned with a person's ability to regulate their emotions. In their study of team problem-solving and emotional intelligence, Jordan and Troth found a correlation between collaborative and dominating styles and emotional intelligence when completing team tasks.[32] They suggested that the emotionally intelligent person may take the lead so as to complete the task on time. However, where high levels of emotional intelligence were present across the team, collaborative strategies may suffice. Performance was enhanced by increased self emotional awareness but not necessarily by dealing with the emotions of others.

Facilitated discussions, exploring cognitive aspects of emotions, can assist conflicting parties to consider their own and the others' emotional experiences. This can lead to a greater understanding of the significance of different issues as well as areas of common ground. Jameson and others argue that increased self-efficacy in the communication of emotional experiences ultimately leads to parties feeling more in control of the process.[33]

Being able to name and own emotions is an important aspect of this process. Confronting avoidance of emotion is more likely to occur in private session.[34]

Prolonged exposure to conflict situations has been linked to distress, anxiety and depression.[35] In the workplace, ongoing negative emotions have impacts on performance, levels of motivation and well-being. A person's perception of whether or not they have been treated fairly will also impact negatively on their willingness to take on extra roles related to organisational citizenship behaviour. Actions such as avoidant and/or vengeful responses are not compatible with expected behaviours in the workplace and can also have a negative influence on other staff and customers. In their study of workplace conflict, negative emotions and performance, Rispens and Demerouti found that psychological detachment was an effective strategy that allowed people to 'cool off' during relationship conflicts and to re-focus cognitive energy on the task to be achieved.[36] They suggested that organisations 'establish norms not to respond immediately to personal disputes' to allow time for this cooling off to occur.[37] Furthermore, they argued that detachment improves well-being and reduces sleep disturbance. Conflicts that are focused on the work being undertaken are often seen to be productive, leading to improved performance and decision-making ability. However, relationship conflicts related to personal and social issues that are not work-related are seen as counterproductive, resulting in decreased team performance and lowered satisfaction.[38]

Social

When the conflict concerns instrumental goals, those adopting aggressive behaviours have been found to be more likely to have successful outcomes in terms of goal achievement, but this is not the case when the dispute is value-based. In conflicts about values, increased use of aggression has been found to more likely to result in increased retaliatory responses and an escalation of the conflict.[39] Aggressive behaviours can be proactive or reactive and often arise from strong emotions of anger and shame.[40] In reactive aggression, behaviours are impulsive and emotional, whereas in proactive aggression they are planned and predatory. This may include acts of violence that are physical, emotional, economic, verbal or controlling of behaviours. Behaviours might include insults or threats intended to deliberately offend, threatening to throw or kick things or actually doing so, and physical acts such as hitting, slapping, pushing, shoving, spitting and biting.[41]

Webb relates aggression in males to their sense of masculinity, distinguishing between 'attack self' behaviours that are related to shame and humiliation in relation to their manhood and 'attack others' behaviours aimed at defending their masculinity. For Webb, shame is 'that sense of disconnect from the world, breakdown of expectations and particularly, break in connection with significant others'.[42] He identifies additional behaviours of 'hide from themselves' or 'hide from others' adopted by those who feel alienated.

Webb contends that 'the culture of shame' is at the heart of violent relationships and not 'the culture of power' that he sees as symptomatic of 'shame guilt', 'shame humiliation' and 'shaming'.[43] He argues that behaviour change strategies aimed at shaming men using cognitive approaches are not likely to succeed and can in fact lead to further violence and alienation. In addition to acts of aggression and violence, other responses to shaming include depression, suicide and self-harm, apathy, isolation, and addictions to alcohol, other substances, work, sex and gambling. Webb suggests that success is more likely to result from the adoption of approaches that encourage men to explore their emotions and 'the abuse power of patriarchy and make conscious decisions to move from behaviours of power and control to ones that are collaborative and egalitarian in relationships'.[44]

Verbal strategies are used to attack, defend and restore face for self and others. People who engage in verbally aggressive behaviours often attack the self-concept of the other person[45] and use more power-based tactics.[46] Verbal aggression is argumentativeness that often involves name-calling and accusations supported by non-verbal behaviours, including physical aggression, violence and abuse aimed at attacking the person's position and often also the person's self-concept while at the same time defending their own position. These deliberately destructive behaviours inflict significant damage upon relationships, causing 'psychological and emotional pain'.[47]

Rogan and La France argue that verbal aggressiveness is deliberately used as a predictable strategy for goal achievement, with little concern for relationships.[48] Congruency, or lack thereof, between verbal and non-verbal behaviours conveys information on emotional states and intentions with the latter being the most reliable.[49] However, it is not always easy to read non-verbal behaviour accurately due to cultural and personal differences. For instance, silence may mean the person is listening, avoiding confrontation or possibly planning a counter-attack.[50] Silence can also be used as a form of aggression that causes aggravation and an escalation of the conflict that could see one person increasingly withdrawing and the other person becoming more demanding.[51]

Infante and colleagues have developed a skill efficiency model that purports that aggressive language reflects a lack of adequate negotiation skills to argue effectively.[52] Others, however, argue that aggressive behaviours are deliberately chosen and can be a 'strategy of first choice' focused on goal achievement aimed at escalating the competitive and distributive aspects of the dispute.[53] In their study of the relationship between verbal aggressiveness, conflict interaction goals and conflict management, Rogan and La France found that verbally aggressive people were not concerned about losing face. The reasons for this were not clear. However, they suggest that it may be that the aggressive person's sense of face was fixed or that perhaps they felt justified that their behaviour was appropriate given the circumstances.

1. *Reflect on what you have done in the past week. Have you revealed private thoughts and emotions to anyone during this time? If yes, what was the relationship with this person? If not, why not?*
2. *What emotions have you experienced so far today? What was happening to make you feel this way?*

Barriers to interpersonal effectiveness

Barriers to engaging in effective interpersonal and public communication include fear and anxiety, shyness and self-blame.[54] Fear and anxiety interfere with effective interpersonal relationships more than any other emotions as they cause avoidance of the anxiety-provoking situation or they immobilise interpersonal interaction within the situation. Learning to overcome fear and anxiety is an essential ingredient of interpersonal effectiveness. A main problem arising from fear and anxiety is shyness. Shyness is expressed in being overly self-conscious and cautious. Shyness can interfere with developing and maintaining, friendships and effective working relationships. Self-blame, the directing of anger towards oneself for not living up to your own or others' hopes and expectations, can further inhibit the development of effective relationships.

Managing anxiety and fear

A range of skills and strategies can assist in effectively managing fear and anxiety. These include accepting fear and anxiety as natural feelings that are to be experienced, not to be fought or resisted. Personal ownership is created by accepting these feelings as legitimate experiences that can be managed rather than as external forces that just happen. This allows for the fear- and anxiety-provoking situation or event to be viewed as a problem to be managed and resolved, not as a catastrophe to hide from. Acceptance of these as natural feelings also reduces the fear of the anxiety itself. Increased self-awareness and self-acceptance can also reduce anxiety.[55]

Learning how to relax systematically, both physically and mentally, can reduce fear and anxiety. This might be simple stretching of muscles that tighten when under stress, as well as deep breathing and positive self talk. A relaxed person cannot be anxious.

Cognitive behaviour therapy techniques for managing fear and anxiety include mindfulness, flooding, systematic desensitisation and guided imagery. Careful matching is required to decide what will work best for a particular person. Personal ownership is also required for the preferred choice of strategies to reduce fear and anxiety. The imposition of these strategies, particularly flooding, by workers or others with good intentions, can lead to disastrous consequences.

Mindfulness focuses on 'being in the moment' and awareness of self and is increasingly used in alternative dispute resolution. The aim is to develop a calm awareness of what is happening with your body, mind and emotions. Meditation is a main technique, as well as simple relaxation strategies. A relatively easy activity is to focus on three consecutive breaths as a conscious experience of mind and body activity.

Flooding is a technique of immersing a person in experiences of what they are most afraid of. Avoidance can often cause fear and anxiety to escalate out of proportion. So flooding may reduce fear and anxiety as the experience might not seem to warrant the level of anxiety that has been provoked by keeping away from it.

Systematic desensitisation is a more gentle and preferred approach, whereby the person is gradually exposed to the source of stress.

Guided imagery is useful for overcoming fears by developing mental images of successfully engaging in the anxiety-provoking behaviour.

Role play simulations are often used to practise facing a fearful situation. This allows for time to think and plan strategies and approaches, as well as examine performance. Changes can then be made to improve performance with opportunities for further practice.

Often, mediators will coach people in effective communication skills so they are better able to participate in the mediation process and negotiate effectively. This frequently includes coaching in assertive behaviours. Assertive behaviours are discussed in more detail in the next chapter.

Eliza was employed as a medical receptionist and her duties included managing the accounts. She had experienced some financial difficulties and found it quite easy to pocket some of this money for herself. Over time, the amount she was taking increased and soon became apparent to her employer. The matter was referred to mediation with role plays used in private sessions with both the employer and Eliza to practise how they might approach each other and what they might say during negotiations. Eliza had been a long-term employee and her employer did not want to press criminal charges against her. An agreement was reached whereby Eliza remained in her employment with a deduction from each week's salary until the debt was paid. Not surprisingly, she was no longer the accounts manager.

1. *What situations make you feel anxious or fearful?*
2. *What do you do to manage your anxiety and fear?*

Culture in communication

Culture refers to the relatively specialised lifestyle of a group of people. It includes values, beliefs, ways of behaving and ways of communicating. While culture generally refers to lifestyle, it is also used to describe other groups of people in work groups, organisations, sporting clubs and associations and so on. The term 'subculture' refers to minority groups within a dominant culture who possess values and beliefs different from those of the dominant culture. Culture is passed on through communication.

Intercultural communication is communication between people

who have different cultural beliefs, values or ways of behaving. Distinctions are often made between individualist and collectivist cultures. Western culture is often seen as individualist, and Eastern and southern European cultures as being more collective. In reality, these are two extremes of the one continuum with all cultures sitting within a particular range. Globalisation and intermarriage between different cultural groups has resulted in a blend of cultures that incorporates aspects of both individualist and collectivist cultures.[56] The distinction is also blurred when cultures are stereotyped as either one or the other, as many cultures that are classified as Western share many similarities to Eastern cultures. For instance, there are many similarities between traditional Chinese, Italian, Irish and Somali cultural values and beliefs, particularly around the importance of the family.

In individual-oriented cultures, the individual's goals are considered most important, with individual accountability and responsibility. Competition is emphasised, with success determined by the individual doing better than others. Personal relationships are less important. Directness is valued and information is explicit.

In collectivist cultures, the group's goals are most important. The individual is responsible to the entire group and the group's values and rules, and success is dependent upon the individual's contribution to the group. Personal relationships are extremely important. Information is often left implicit and much is often omitted from explicit statements. Indirectness is valued and face-saving is a major consideration.

Sometimes, people are fearful of working with others who are culturally different, as they think they do not have sufficient knowledge and understanding of a particular culture to work effectively. It is important to face these fears and to recognise and understand cultural factors that are relevant to the conflict. In some instances, people are referred to ethno-specific agencies for specialist information and support. Often, these agencies are not well funded and cannot provide the range of services available to the community through mainstream services. A more appropriate way of working is for agencies to work together and for mainstream services to employ workers from a variety of cultures who speak a range of community languages.

Principles for effective intercultural mediation include allowing extra time for preparation to become familiar with the cultural values and beliefs of the people you are working with and behaving in a manner that is respectful of cultural rules and customs. At the same time, it is important to avoid stereotyping and also to recognise differences among those who are culturally different. These may be differences within a family according to the generation to which the family member belongs. Differences also occur across cultures in the meanings of verbal and non-verbal messages.[57]

Troung, an eighteen-year-old man of Vietnamese background, was charged with minor offences and summoned to appear in the local magistrate's court. As a sign of respect, he looked down at the ground when the magistrate addressed him and did not at any stage make eye contact with him. Within Vietnamese culture, lack of eye contact is deemed a mark of respect. However, the magistrate interpreted this as Troung being guilty and unrepentant and gave him a harsh sentence.

It is often tempting to use family members as interpreters to save time and money. This can be at a considerable cost to relationships and the conflict management process, as the information is not always translated correctly. This may be due to a range of reasons. For instance, in Chinese culture, it is considered bad luck to deliver bad news to a person, particularly if they are older than you. It is also rude to refuse to pass on a message if asked to do so by a worker. This necessarily results in a modified message being conveyed in an indirect way.[58] It is necessary to use appropriately skilled interpreters and learn how to work effectively with them.

A doctor was using a son, who had excellent English ability, to interpret to his elderly parents who only spoke Mandarin. The doctor asked the son to tell his father he had a terminal illness. The son spoke to his father but did not pass on the message, as it was culturally inappropriate to do so. The doctor was unaware that this communication was not conveyed.

1. *List the main cultural influences in your own life. Are they more individual or collective?*
2. *What contact do you currently have with people from cultures that are different to your own? Describe some of the similarities and difference you have become aware of.*

Communication activity

The purpose of this exercise is to increase sensitivity to attending behaviours in general and to get some idea of what your attending skills are like in your daily interactions with others.

1. *Observe a social interaction focusing on non-verbal communications. Position yourself so you are not listening to them. Describe the interaction and comment specifically on*
    – posture
    – gestures
    – facial expressions
    List all non-verbal behaviour from the neck, head and face.
    List all non-verbal behaviour from the arms and hands.
    List all non-verbal behaviour from the whole body.
2. *Observe an interview, preferably with a politician, on a television news or current affairs program. Apply the same criteria above. Check for congruency between verbal and non-verbal content.*
3. *Observe the quality of your presence with others during the week monitoring use of verbal and non-verbal attending behaviours. To whom are you most attentive and in what context?*
    Note that when asked to observe your own behaviours, you are likely to change them and probably use more effective attending behaviours than usual.

Conclusion

Conflict is a normal everyday experience. Self-reflection and an understanding of the roles people play in conflict assists in analysing conflict and managing it effectively. The ways people communicate with each other are influenced by a number of personal and social factors. Life experience and personality type will influence perceptions of others and their circumstances and expectations. Emotions are an important aspect of communication in conflict situations as they reflect personal experiences of events. In conflict management and mediation, emotions are often overlooked, with a focus instead on process and content. Effective conflict management strategies acknowledge emotions as an important aspect of the conflict. Fear and anxiety, shyness and self-blame can often present as barriers to effective communication. Acknowledgement of these as legitimate feelings allows for them to be viewed as part of a problem to be managed or resolved. Likewise, acknowledgement of and respect for different cultural beliefs, values and ways of behaving are essential for effective cross-cultural communication. Effective communication and conflict management strategies strengthen relationships by facilitating greater depth of understanding and commitment.

Chapter 2 takes a closer look at understanding conflict and the ways people behave in conflict situations.

2

Understanding Conflict

People interpret conflict situations differently, attaching their own meanings and interpretations to events. These events evoke a range of responses and reactions. Some common responses are referred to as 'fight' and 'flight' responses. Flight responses are the same as the avoidance behaviours discussed in the previous chapter. This chapter focuses on developing a greater understanding of conflict. A closer look is taken at how a person's behaviour may change according to the nature and level of the conflict. Different types of conflict management processes are presented and consideration given to issues of power. The notion of cooperative power is presented as a useful strategy in conflict management. Skills and techniques in assertive behaviours are presented and consideration given to issues in worker self-care.

Levels of conflict

It is not unusual for people to change the way they behave in conflict situations in accordance with the nature and level of the conflict. The nature of the conflict refers to the contextual factors within which the conflict is occurring. This will determine the significance of the conflict, personal and emotional involvement, and possible impacts. Levels of conflict refer to the stage the conflict is at. Generally, if interventions occur at the early stages, the conflict is more easily resolved. However, professional assistance for conflict resolution is usually sought only when the conflict is long-standing and entrenched.

Often in conflict situations, an incident occurs that causes anxiety.

This can result in misinterpretation if differences are not discussed or clarified. Problems may arise in terms of trust and respect, leading to negative expectations and heightened levels of anxiety. This is particularly problematic when close and ongoing communications are required, such as teamwork and parenting. Depending upon personality type, discussed in chapter 1, either outbursts or silences can occur, causing further harm to relationships. This cycle often continues, with patterns of miscommunication becoming more and more entrenched and damaging.

Figure 2.1[1]

Cycle of Conflict

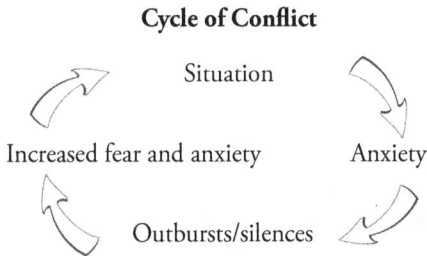

The conflict often impacts on others not directly involved. For example, if two members in a work team are constantly at war, it affects the operations of the entire team and, ultimately, productivity. Often, the parties are so preoccupied with their own issues and sense of being wronged that they have no idea of the impact on the other person in the conflict and on innocent third parties.

Behaviours in conflict situations can be broadly classified into five categories:

– collaborative
– compromising
– accommodating
– avoiding, and
– forcing.[2]

Response is influenced by how the conflict situation is viewed. A person who is collaborative will welcome differences and encourage the sharing of ideas and views. Mutual agreement is sought that meets as many needs and concerns of all parties as possible. Compromise is also a conciliatory approach that acknowledges difference, and responds by finding a mid-point between the differences; this is often an equal sharing. Accommodating behaviours tend to avoid conflict by favouring the other person's views in an endeavour to avoid conflict. The interests of the accommodating person are often forgone and can result in heightened levels of anxiety. Avoiding behaviours delay or prevent a response. This may be by diversion, withdrawal or refusal to engage. Forcing is coercion to the views of one or more party over the others. The conflict focuses on who is 'right' and who is 'wrong'.

As already mentioned, responses vary according to the level the conflict is at. It is worthwhile being aware of your own responses, and how these might change according to the intensity of the conflict. It is also useful to consider how behaviours of people you are working with may change according to the level of conflict. When behaviours change, the person may be seen as unpredictable or erratic. However, often what is being expressed is a different response to a contextual change that has altered the level of the conflict. For instance, the person may be accommodating when low levels of anxiety are present but forceful when levels of anxiety and fear increase. In this situation, an amicable response may change to 'Enough is enough. Now we'll do it my way' for seemingly no apparent reason.

1. *How do you think, feel and behave when you hear the word conflict?*
2. *Think of a recent conflict situation: how did you behave when the conflict first began?*
3. *How did you behave when the conflict intensified?*

Different types of conflict resolution

Increasingly, conflict resolution is being called by different names, sometimes without any change to the actual practice. For instance, in the early

1990s, in Australia, 'alternative dispute resolution' was the favoured term and was synonymous with mediation. 'Alternative' was used to distinguish mediation as an alternative to litigation. However, over the past two decades, courts and tribunal have taken on an increasing role in broadening the range and opportunities for conflict resolution, and in many cases mediation is mandated by a court before a case is listed for hearing. Rather than an alternative to litigation, mediation has become a part of the judicial system. In family disputes, alternative dispute resolution has been replaced with 'family dispute resolution' and is also known as 'primary dispute resolution'. In essence, the practices are the same but the context has changed. A range of mediation models has developed, with conflict now taking place among dispute resolution practitioners as to what model is the best. These models are discussed in chapter 4.

The main types of conflict resolution are litigation, arbitration, conciliation, facilitation, co-mediation and mediation, and negotiation. The level of involvement and power over the decision making process by the disputing parties can be seen on a continuum from greatest power with negotiation, to least power in litigation where a decision is handed down. This is illustrated in figure 2.2.

Figure 2.2

Power over outcome by disputing parties

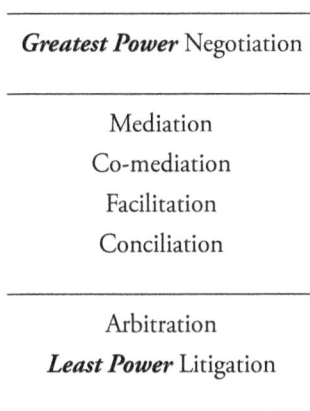

Greatest Power Negotiation

Mediation
Co-mediation
Facilitation
Conciliation

Arbitration
Least Power Litigation

Negotiation occurs directly between two parties. If they are unable to reach a decision, a third party may attempt to promote communication; this is referred to as 'assisted negotiation'.

In mediation, a neutral third party manages a dispute resolution process based on a win/win approach to assist the parties to reach a future focused agreement.

In co-mediation, two mediators assist the parties.

Facilitation is usually conducted with small groups. The facilitator assists with problem identification and tasks to be accomplished. A facilitator may also assist by developing options and endeavouring to reach an agreement between the disputing parties. A main focus of facilitation, however, is on managing a process rather than achieving outcomes.

In conciliation, the focus is also on developing options and considering alternatives. The conciliator has an expert advisory role and may actively encourage the parties to reach an agreement.

The main difference between arbitration and the other dispute resolution methods is that an arbitrator can make legally binding decisions, after consideration of the arguments and evidence presented by the parties.

In litigation, a magistrate or judge or jury will decide.

The balance of power is fundamental to the appropriateness, and ultimate success, of any attempted conflict resolution process. Assessment of the degree to which power imbalances are present, and the ability and willingness of parties to enter into discussions on equal terms, will influence the choice of the most appropriate conflict resolution process, and ultimately outcomes.

In pairs:
Stand facing a partner and form a handshake.
Guide your partner's hand to your opposite hip.
Score one point each time you do this successfully.
Count how many points you score in one minute.

Cooperative power

Cooperative power involves sharing power and not exerting power over others. The notion of cooperative power stems from feminist theory and is particularly relevant to leadership in groups and organisations as well as interpersonal relationships. It is necessary to have an understanding of power generally as well as personal power. Critical theory is discussed in chapter 3 and is particularly useful in analysing power relationships in conflict according to dominant social, economic and political forces. A focus is on ability, age, class, gender, race, ethnicity and culture, sexuality and spirituality.

1. *Who has power over you?*
2. *Who do you have power over?*
3. *Who do you feel powerful around and in what settings?*
4. *How do you give away your power?*
5. *Think of a person who you often defer to or whose requests you usually comply with. What is this power to get agreement and cooperation from you based on?*

Often, we agree with another person because of a valued relationship, recognition of expertise or persuasiveness. On the other hand, agreement may also be motivated by more negative influences, such as the desire to be rewarded or to avoid punishment. Such behaviours often results in the person left feeling coerced or manipulated.

It is useful to consider the difference between manipulation and influence. Manipulation can stunt relationships and result in people feeling tricked or in extreme cases bullied. Often, biased information is presented that favours the view of the manipulator and her or his preferred outcomes at the expense of others. Input from others is discouraged and their interests, needs and concerns are less likely to be considered. This generally results in less commitment from all parties to making the solution work.

Influence is the opposite of manipulation. Influence builds relationships because people feel persuaded. Balanced information that considers the interests, needs and concerns of others is presented. Input is encouraged and valued, with outcomes that favour others, not just the influencer. The result is greater commitment by all parties to making the solution work.

Relationships in conflict

In relationships where there is conflict people tend to be portrayed as

- aggressors
- victims, and
- rescuers.[3]

It is important to ascertain whether these behaviours are actually happening, or if parties are being portrayed in these ways as power play. For instance, a person can be described as aggressive and uncooperative, when in reality they are simply expressing a point of view that is different from the person making the accusation. In such instances, the person who is claiming to be the victim is in fact the aggressor. It is useful to distinguish when a person is 'playing' a role for particular gain or advantage.

Aggressive behaviours are used when people are coercing or manipulating others. These behaviours include bullying, putting others down, force, coercion, rewards and punishments.

A person may be a genuine victim or perhaps 'playing victim'. Careful assessment is required to ascertain this. Playing victim behaviours include acting helpless, and talking and acting as if everyone is against them. Claims of inadequacy and hopelessness and defeat are expressed. A person who is playing victim can in fact be very powerful and not as helpless as they seem.

Rescuing behaviours are engaged in by those who deny their own personal needs and constantly help and support others by solving their problems for them. Rescuers act like martyrs and provide a buffer between the parties in conflict. This can be a very stressful place to be.

Power game triangle[4]

Divide into groups of three to conduct the following role play scenario. You will do this scenario three times — each time assuming a different role: aggressor, playing victim or rescuer.

Allow three minutes for each role play.

Role play scenario

Three staff members have to settle on a time for their weekly meeting.

Person 1: You want to meet at 10.30 a.m. You like the flexibility this job offers and do not like afternoon meetings as you collect your children after school and continue your work at home.

Person 2: You want to meet late in the afternoon. You are not a morning person, preferring to arrive at work after the peak hour traffic in the morning and leave later in the day, avoiding the end of the day rush as well. You do not have children but do have a dog that you care dearly about.

Person 3: You want to meet at 9 a.m. You like to get meetings out of the way early on so you can focus on the rest of your work for the remainder of the day. You find this to be the most efficient way of managing your work time.

	Person 1	**Person 2**	**Person 3**
Role play 1	Aggressive	Rescuing	Playing victim
Role play 2	Playing victim'	Aggressive	Rescuing
Role play 3	Rescuing	Playing victim	Aggressive

On a scale of 1 to 5, with 1 being least powerful and 5 being most powerful, score yourself for each role.

1. *How powerful or powerless do you feel in each role?*

   Aggressive: 1 2 3 4 5

   Playing victim: 1 2 3 4 5

   Rescuer: 1 2 3 4 5

2. *Which role did you enjoy the most and why?*

3. *Which role did you enjoy the least and why?*

Consider levels of comfort with each role and what roles you mostly as-
sume in your day-to-day interactions with others.

Behaviour in conflict situations

People behave differently in conflict situations. Some people will deal
with a problem while others avoid it. How a problem is dealt with will
influence whether the relationship is harmed or enhanced. Due to habit
and learnt patterns, people behave in certain ways in conflict situations
according to mood, setting, relationship and significance of the conflict.
Whether a person's belief system is based on the premise that to win
someone else must lose will also affect their approach to conflict.

Behaviours in conflict situations are typically categorised as fight,
flight or assertive. Fight and flight behaviours are often spontaneous reactions to primitive urges; assertive responses are learnt and require a
more reasoned approach. Fight responses include screaming, physical
violence, refusing to listen, manipulation and sulking. The main messages of fight behaviours are 'I'm right, therefore you're wrong' and 'I'm
okay but you're not'. Main intentions are to blame, punish and threaten.

Flight behaviours include sulking, crying, avoiding, pretending the
conflict hasn't happened and giving in. Main messages of flight behaviours are 'I'm wrong, therefore you're right' and 'I'm not okay but
you are'. The main intentions are to avoid conflict, maintain peace and
to let the other person win.

Assertive or 'flow' behaviours include discussing the issue, listening
to others, taking time out and articulating perspective and needs. Main
messages of assertive or flow behaviours are 'There must be a way to
solve this' and 'I'm okay and you're okay'. The main intentions are to
respect others and to make sure everyone is satisfied with the solution.

Assertive statements are often referred to as 'I' statements. Assertive
responses are respectful and start with 'I' rather than 'You', associated
with more aggressive and accusatory interactions. Body language and
tone of voice are particularly important, as well as the content of what
is actually said.

It is important to remain calm but it is also vital to respond in a manner that is appropriate to the seriousness of the situation. For instance, it is not appropriate to appear relaxed and cheerful if the person you are talking with is extremely agitated. You do not want to give the impression that you fail to appreciate the significance of what is happening. Timing and venue are important, so that the person is able to listen and focus on what is being said. 'I' statements and 'running record' are the two main assertiveness techniques.

Assertive statements

A simple assertive response starts with 'When' and then describes the offending behaviour. 'I' is used instead of 'You' to signify ownership of the problem and also to avoid an aggressive response. The offending behaviour, associated feelings and context are shared with the other person.

'When............... I feel .... because ....
(behaviour)   (emotion)   (reason)

An example might go like this: 'When the meetings we schedule to work on our group assignment don't happen, I feel really frustrated because my time at university is so limited outside of normal class hours due to paid work commitments.'

Assertive statements can be varied to suit personal styles and promote conversation flow so long as the basic principles are followed.

Running record

Running record is an assertiveness technique that involves repeating the same response over and over again even though different reasons or arguments may be put to you.

For example, a co-worker asks to borrow some money. This person usually doesn't pay you back and you really don't want to lend them anything. The conversation goes as follows.

'Hi, can you lend me $20 just until tomorrow?'

'Sorry, but I haven't got any spare money I can lend you.'

'Just $10 will do. You see, I'm really desperate – I left my wallet at home.'

'Sorry, but I haven't got any spare money I can lend you.'

'I don't know how I'm going to get home tonight. I haven't got any money for my bus fare home.'

'Sorry, but I don't have any spare money I can lend you.'

'I haven't had any lunch. I'm so hungry and I haven't got any money to buy something!'

'Sorry, but I don't have any spare money I can lend you.'

Usually, repeating the same statement two or three times is enough. Of course, you may change your mind but if you don't, this technique usually works.

> Jasmine was arrested by the police following an altercation at a shopping centre and taken to the police cells. When I walked into the interview room to speak with Jasmine, she threw a cup filled with water at me, swearing and shouting abuse. I assertively told her that I would like to help her if I could but that she needed to cooperate and behave appropriately. I asked her to pick up the cup off the floor before I would speak with her. She sat and looked at me and then swore again telling me to pick it up myself. I repeated the same assertive statement, telling Jasmine that I wanted to help her and hear what had happened but that I needed her to work with me, and again asked her to pick up the cup. This was said in a kind yet firm manner. Jasmine proceeded to pick up the cup and we sat down together and talked.

Assertive behaviours were helpful in setting limits on Jasmine's behaviour and forming a respectful working relationship with her. In this instance, repeating the same message twice was enough.

1. *Think of a person you have difficulty being assertive with. How do you usually behave when you are with her or him?*
2. *Think of a recent situation when you were with this person. Describe this situation to a partner and then act this out in a role play behaving in your usual manner. Repeat this scenario again in*

a second role play but replace your usual response with assertive
behaviours. Practise both 'I' statements and running record.

3. *How did the other person respond to your behaviour in each role*
   play? How did you feel?

Take it in turns to do this exercise.

Difficult behaviours

Often, mediators are confronted with behaviours that are difficult to handle. Depending on our responses we may find ourselves reinforcing these behaviours, giving way or engaging in a power struggle.

Behaviour has a purpose with the fundamental goals of

– being secure
– finding a place of significance
– to belong, and
– to protect one's sense of identity.

When people feel discouraged and threatened, they may replace these fundamental goals with other goals. This may occur subconsciously. They may convince themselves that the only way of getting what they want is to behave in ways that others find difficult. It is the way that others respond to these behaviours that will influence whether or not these behaviours persist. The four goals of difficult behaviours identified by Rudolph Dreikurs and associated behaviours are presented in figure 2.3.

Figure 2.3

Goals of difficult behaviour[5]

Goal	Behaviours
Gaining attention	being loud, fidgeting, asking lots of questions, being stubborn, sick, clumsy, over-helpful or over-nice or chatting inappropriately

Gaining power	interrupting, putting others down, being critical, manipulative, giving advice, gathering allies
Appearing inadequate	avoiding, procrastinating, apologising, forgetful, submissive, getting it wrong, self-depreciating 'I can't', shirking responsibilities
Seeking revenge	sabotaging, sulking, withholding information, backstabbing, withholding praise and privileges, excluding others, one-upping, harm and violence

If considered on a continuum, these behaviours are listed from the easiest to most difficult to manage. Attention-seeking behaviours can result in a brief feeling of sense of significance, particularly when a person is receiving lots of attention. By gaining power through negative behaviours, a person may feel secure when bossing and controlling others. When displaying apparent inadequacy, a person may feel they belong if others look after them, as in the case of playing victim. A person may seek to maintain his or her sense of identity by seeking revenge and inflicting hurt and provoking hostility. One or more of these four goals may be used to get the mediator onside. This might be by using attention-seeking behaviours such as being overly nice or perhaps appearing inadequate and appealing to the mediator for rescue.

Preferred responses to these goals of difficult behaviours are presented in figure 2.4.

Figure 2.4

Responding to difficult behaviours

Goal	Response
Gaining attention	Ignore
Gaining power	Withdraw
Appearing inadequate	Encourage
Seeking revenge	Don't retaliate

Attention-seeking behaviours are best managed by ignoring them and acknowledging and rewarding positive behaviours and contributions. However, if such behaviours are disturbing the mediation process, it is the role of the mediator to manage them. This is generally done by reminding parties of the process and mediation rules that have been agreed on at the outset. Sometimes, a party is spoken to privately if the disruptive behaviours persist, and in extreme situations the mediation may not continue. These two latter actions are more likely to be caused by behaviours aimed at gaining power or revenge rather than attention-seeking; these are generally more easily managed.

When a power struggle develops, it is often best to withdraw. This is not the same as giving up. It is more a matter of approaching the conflict in a different way rather than going head to head with an adversary. A competitor in a power struggle relies on having an opponent to defeat. By removing the challenger from the situation, the conflict is necessarily diffused.

Appearing inadequate behaviours are best managed by encouragement and reinforcement of efforts to engage in positive and assertive behaviours. If a person is seeking revenge or has engaged in retaliation, it is important that the other party does not retaliate, as this will escalate the conflict. It is the role of the mediator to explore the negative impacts of such behaviours and to encourage more appropriate and conciliatory responses.

Self-care

Working in conflict management can be very interesting and rewarding. It can also be very stressful. These stressors can arise from working in high-demand and complex settings, such as working with people who are misusing substances, mentally unwell, violent and engaged in offending, or a combination of these. Stressors can be exacerbated by high workloads and colleagues who can also pose difficult and challenging behaviours. I recall my initiation into the disability services workforce as a new graduate being asked in my first week of employment, by a colleague with a wry smile, if I had found the gift she had left for me: a pile of faeces in an unflushed toilet. I was shocked and did not share the incident with anyone at the time.

Stress can result in the development of physical, psychological and behavioural issues that can impact upon our ability to look after ourselves, let alone the people we are working with. Prolonged high stress can result in burnout that has serious detrimental effects not only on work performance and satisfaction but also on a person's health and well-being and personal relationships. In the workplace, this often results in increased sick leave days and higher staff turnover. On the home front, it can contribute to relationship breakdowns, and heath and mental health issues arising from disillusionment, despair, anxiety and fear. This is serious, and workplaces can no longer ignore the negative demands of the workplace on the well-being of their staff.

In a recent landmark case in the state of Victoria, Australia, the manager of a truck company was charged with manslaughter following the death of four police officers who were hit and killed by a truck driven by a company employee. The manager was charged with safety breaches related to driver fatigue and use of trucks in need of repairs. This provides a clear warning and precedent to other employers that they are responsible at law for providing employees with a safe work environment.

Workers often do not complain, as they worry about getting offside with their manager. This can be exacerbated for people in casual and irregular employment and particularly those from immigrant non-English-speaking backgrounds. Those working in the so-called helping professions can want very much to please others, become upset when hearing of the difficult circumstances of others and may blame the client or organisation for the emotional distress they carry. Human service workers are complaining of vicarious trauma from having to listen to the distressing stories of the lives of their clients. This is really problematic for the worker, those they work with and the human services professions. I cannot imagine what it must be like for a client to open up and share traumatic events that they have actually lived through with a worker who then in turn becomes traumatised.

This all points to the importance of worker self-care and developing the ability to take control of our own feelings and emotions, to keep things in perspective, to speak up and ask for assistance when required, to work collaboratively with others, and to understand that it is not reasonable to be emotionally overwhelmed by a client's circumstances if we are going to provide appropriate professional assistance and self-care. This is not to undermine worker responses but to say we need to look after ourselves to be able to look after our clients.

Self-care is important to maintain positive physical and mental health, and well-being. This includes adequate rest and relaxation, diet, exercise, taking time out when necessary, mentoring, supervision and continuing professional development. This in turn influences the quality of your presence with others, as discussed in the previous chapter. Employers are responsible for providing formal supervision, debriefing and staff development, a manageable workload and accessible and experienced senior staff to assist with difficult situations. However, sole practitioners are not likely to have access to the same level of support and resources and must source them privately.

Effective mediator self-care requires self-awareness and self-monitoring to identify situations that trigger strong emotional responses. This includes what is said and tone of voice, as well as what is not said but rather observed through body language and behaviour. Professional supervision is extremely important, even for experienced workers, as it provides an opportunity to reflect on situations, gain perspective and increase skills to do things differently next time. Sometimes, workers are not confident to seek professional supervision from managers due to fear of being seen as not competent and limiting opportunities. If this is the case, professional supervision will need to be sought externally from the organisation. Continuing professional education to further develop advanced skills can increase competency and improve attitudes, flexibility and outcomes. Managing workload can assist in balancing the number of difficult clients seen in one day with others who are generally less challenging as well as managing overall caseload numbers that are realistic and reasonable.

Worker safety is paramount and should not be knowingly compromised. Mediators always need to be aware of entry and exit points; preferred venues should have multiple entry and exit points that can be easily accessed. In situations of possible violence, main skills include remaining calm, appropriate body language, listening and assertiveness, while providing adequate physical space between yourself and the person. Respect for personal space is required, with the potentially threatening person in a position where, if they choose to leave, they can easily get past the mediator. At the same time, it is wise for the mediators to sit close to the door for an easy exit if danger arises, or is suspected. However, it is important that others have a clear pathway past you so they can also leave freely. If a person feels threatened or trapped, they are more likely to be violent.

Efforts are required to engage the person so that they see the mediator as an ally. Moving the topic of discussion to one that is less upsetting or threatening is a useful strategy as well as setting boundaries. Too many questions may aggravate a person who is already agitated. Focusing on the content and shifting the topic can assist the person to regain control of difficult emotions while letting them know the mediators are still on side.

Mediations which are anticipated to be difficult require thorough planning and preparation and the allocation of two mediators. However, it is often in mediations that seem relatively straightforward that unanticipated problems can arise. The message is to be thorough in all of your planning and preparations. Mediator neutrality, location and design of the meeting venue are all important, particularly if violence is an issue.[5] A balance needs to be struck between need for privacy and comfort and safety.

Strategies for avoiding and preventing potentially dangerous or violent situations involve preparation and assessment, as well as practical measures such as letting office staff and others know where you are going and when you will return, as well as carrying a mobile telephone. It is important to trust personal reactions of discomfort and to explore their source. Mediation should not proceed if weapons are known to be present or danger is suspected. Mediation sessions should not be conducted with parties who are under the influence of alcohol and other drugs. This may not be known immediately but if a person's behaviour or judgement is seen to be altered by substances, the mediation session should be discontinued.

Mediators can use the process of breaking for private session, and during that time remove one party before seeing the other party. The mediators may seek assistance from supervisors and colleagues as well as endeavour to get assistance from a close associate of the aggressor who may be able to assist. In situations of extreme danger, police involvement may be necessary, and proper briefing essential.

Once the situation is resolved, it is important that appropriate professional supervision and debriefing is provided as soon as possible. Unfortunately, workers are often blamed for difficult situations that arise and debriefing and supervision can turn into an attack on the mediator, both personally and professionally. It is important that the mediator is listened to and supported in trying to understand what has happened and looking at ways to prevent and manage similar situations that may arise in the future.

A number of strategies can be put in place to prevent and manage difficult and potentially violent situations, but they can also arise quite unexpectedly. However, if such strategies are in place, mediators are less likely to be caught off guard in the same way I was with John.

John was twenty years of age and had recently broken up with his girlfriend Kelly, who had started going out with his best mate. He was referred to mediation by his father, who felt that John was not coping well with the break-up. According to John's father, John kept contacting Kelly and refused to accept that she no longer wanted to even talk to him. John's father felt that a mediation session with John and

Kelly would help John to move on and at the same time stop him from bothering Kelly.

I contacted John and arranged an intake meeting with him. He told me he had just started a new job and could only attend of an evening. I arranged an appointment late in the day. John was a pleasant yet intense young man. I told him that the purpose of our meeting was to determine the suitability of mediation between him and Kelly. I also mentioned to John that whatever he told me was confidential unless I was concerned about his or others' safety.

John went on to tell me about Kelly and how much he had loved her and hoped one day to marry her. He became quite upset and agitated when talking about how Kelly had left him and was now with his best mate. He became very angry and was crying uncontrollably. He was extremely jealous to the point of rage. He told me if he couldn't have Kelly, no one would, and proceeded to tell me he had access to a gun and planned to kill them both.

I told John I was concerned about him and also his threats towards Kelly and her new boyfriend. I then told him I needed to discuss it with others who could assist. John turned his anger towards me and said what he had said was in confidence and I was to tell no one. My immediate thought was 'Oh no, I think I'm here in the building alone with John.' I was right – everyone else had left for the day and here we were alone and quite isolated on the seventh floor. John was verbally abusive and stormed out.

I called John's father and told him what had happened and the threats John had made and his plans. John's father located and removed the gun and arranged for the family doctor to see John that evening to arrange an immediate referral to counselling. John's father agreed to keep a close watch over him for the next couple of days.

In hindsight, it was unwise to see John alone after hours. The referral should have alerted me to his anger. That he was a young male could heighten that. More skilled intervention could have occurred to get John to explore the consequences of his actions. I should have appeared to work with him rather than be seen as acting against him by breaching his confidence. John's lack of ability to control his emotions and the rate at which they escalated was a warning that he needed assistance to deal with their intensity. A greater focus on content and distracting him onto more practical information about his work and sport might have assisted. Often, people will make threats to intimidate others yet not act on them. John's situation was one where the threats were treated seriously because he had a well-developed plan and the means to enact it. It is not always easy to know how to respond particularly when the threats are made towards you as a mediator or co-workers.

Ria was a young woman who was diagnosed with borderline personality disorder. She was referred to mediation by the police due to conflict with neighbours and threats she had made towards them. One neighbour was frightened to let her children play in the yard because she was scared Ria would harm them. I saw Ria at her home for an intake assessment of her suitability for mediation.

Later that day, Ria called me and started swearing, telling me she knew I had a child at a day care centre and she was going to kill it. I listened carefully to Ria and realised she did not know the sex of my child or where she was. While the threats were disturbing, she did not have a detailed plan in the same way John had. The threats were more an indication to me of Ria's general distress and the difficulties she was having.

However, I did find working with Ria difficult, particularly her self-harming and threatening behaviours. On one occasion, she hid in a toilet cubicle at our centre and jumped over the divider onto another social worker who was on the toilet. The worker complained bitterly about this and blamed me for not managing Ria's difficult behaviours. At times I was quite frightened of Ria but, instead of offers of assistance from colleagues, I was faced with their anger and resentment.

It was clear to me that Ria needed assistance with daily living in the community and managing living with a mental illness and intellectual disability. She also needed boundaries to help her contain what were often very difficult behaviours. The extreme nature of her behaviours and the fact that she had been referred by the police suggested that if appropriate assistance was not provided by health and community services, Ria would eventually end up in the criminal justice system.

1. *Can you work effectively with someone you are scared of?*
2. *Do you think it is appropriate to conduct a mediation session with someone who has a mental illness and/or intellectual disability? Provide reasons.*
3. *Can you think of other things you might do for self-care in addition to those mentioned?*

Conclusion

A number of factors influence how conflict is prevented, managed or resolved. These include the context and significance of the conflict, and the level or stage that the conflict has reached. Main types of conflict resolution are litigation, arbitration, conciliation, facilitation, mediation and negotiation. Litigation and arbitration are adversarial; the remaining approaches are less formal and more conciliatory. An analysis of power relationships is central to conflict management. In relationships where there is conflict, people are often portrayed as aggressors, victims and rescuers. It is important for mediators to assess if these behaviours are actually happening or if parties are being portrayed as such due to power play. Behaviours in conflict situations are typically categorised as fight or flight or assertive. The first two are instinctive reactions, and assertiveness is a learnt response. Assertiveness and listening skills are essential for effective communication in the mediation process by both the mediator and the conflicting parties. Self-care is important when working in conflict management and mediation. It is important that staff receive appropriate support through supervision, debriefing and staff development, and have workloads that are manageable.

3

Mediation

Mediation, also known as alternative dispute resolution or, more recently, as primary dispute resolution, is one of the main approaches to conflict resolution. As mentioned in chapter 2, mediation is one of many conflict resolution processes, including litigation, arbitration, facilitation, conciliation and negotiation. All are designed to steer would-be litigants away from the legal process. Increasingly, however, mediation is being used as the preferred process. Mediation can be implemented before or during other dispute resolution processes such as litigation or arbitration. The naming of these combined practices reflects the approach taken. For instance, med-arb is used to describe a process that combines mediation and arbitration.

Mediation is an ancient art practised in the earliest Chinese dynasties as a way of promoting and maintaining social cohesion. Until the twenty-first century, mediation was generally seen as a voluntary process. However, in recent years there has been a considerable increase in the use of mandatory mediation in a number of different areas, particularly in family and criminal, and building and planning disputes. Increasingly, people attend mediation because they have been directed to do so by a court or tribunal or due to a contractual arrangement that requires the use of alternative dispute resolution processes.[1] The court or tribunal or contract may stipulate how the alternative dispute process is to be conducted and this generally includes 'acting in good faith'.

Mediation is a process conducted in private, where the parties to a dispute meet to resolve their differences with the assistance of a neutral third-party mediator. The mediator manages the mediation process, assisting parties to identify the issues in the dispute, develop options, consider alternatives and endeavour to reach agreement. The mediation process is future-focused. Unlike a conciliator, the mediator does not provide any expert information or advice on possible solutions.[2] Conciliation is often preferred to mediation in planning disputes when the mediator is from a planning background.

This chapter explores the main models of mediation and dispute resolution. The principle of win/win that underpins most models is discussed, as well as the mutual gains approach to negotiation. Main features of the mediation process are identified, as well as required skills. Ethical consideration and practice standards are also discussed.

Models of mediation

Mediation is defined as follows:

> Mediation is a confidential process where an independent and neutral third party assists the disputants to negotiate and reach a decision about their dispute. Unlike arbitration, or expert appraisal, the mediator cannot impose a decision upon the parties. However, through their facilitation and technical skill, the mediator is able to assist the parties to explore the issues in depth and reach the best possible joint decisions that the circumstances allow.[3]

Mediation is a process where the participants, with the assistance of an independent person as mediator,

- listen to and are heard by each other
- work out what the disputed issues are
- work out what is important to each person
- aim to reach a workable agreement
- develop options to resolve each issue
- develop options that take into account each person's needs and desires, and

– discuss what everyone could do as a way of assessing the options and exploring what might lead to an outcome that everyone can live with.[4]

Participants in mediation are advised,

A mediator can help you and the other participants have a respectful, even-handed discussion and decision making process. Your role is to listen to the other points of view, contribute to the discussion and make decisions. Mediation may be voluntary, court ordered, or required as part of a contract or external dispute resolution arrangement.[5]

Familiarity with legislation particular to the nature of the dispute is required to ensure that mediation and dispute resolution practice complies with legislative provisions and requirements. Legislation includes professional qualifications required of mediators to practise in certain areas, supervision and continuing professional development arrangements. The mediator must ensure that agreements made at mediation are within the law.

Different models of mediation include settlement, facilitative, evaluative and therapeutic mediation.[6] Newer models are narrative mediation, transformative mediation, preventative mediation, policy-making mediation and collaborative family law. In legal settings, therapeutic mediation is often referred to as therapeutic jurisprudence; international dispute resolution is referred to as international jurisprudence. Different models suit different types of disputes. In practice, mediation may include elements of more than one of these models. The main objectives and characteristic features of each of these models and areas of practice suitability are described below.

Settlement mediation is also known as compromise mediation. The main objective is to encourage incremental bargaining in an endeavour to reach a compromise at a mid-point of the demands of both parties. The dispute is defined in terms of the parties' definition of the problem and their positions. Applicable areas of practice include commercial, personal injury, victims of crime and workplace disputes.

Facilitative mediation is also known as interest-based, problem-solving mediation. The main objective is to negotiate in terms of the parties' needs and interests as opposed to legal entitlements.[7] Creative problem-solving techniques are used in the negotiation phase to find a win/win solution that satisfies most of the needs of all the parties to the dispute.[8] Areas of practice include community, family, relationship, parent–adolescent, adult–elder and environmental disputes.

Evaluative mediation is also known as advisory, managerial mediation. The main objective is to reach a settlement in accordance with the legal rights and entitlements of the parties. The dispute is defined in terms of legal rights, duties, industry standards and community norms. Precedents may be used to inform parties of the way that courts have decided similar matters in the past.[9] Areas of practice include commercial, personal injury, anti-discrimination, trade practices and property disputes.

Preventative mediation focuses on anticipating conflict and establishing processes that can be used to assist parties to identify difficult and often complex issues and to develop processes for dealing with them. In this manner, conflict is pre-empted and strategies are in place to both prevent conflict and deal with it constructively when it does occur.

The main objective of therapeutic mediation is to improve relationships between parties by dealing with underlying causes of conflict as a basis for resolving the dispute. The dispute is defined in terms of relationships, emotions and behaviours. This is particularly suited to areas of practice where continuing interpersonal relationships are important, such as marital, family, parent–adolescent, and adult–elder.

Narrative mediation, an approach that originated in New Zealand, also focuses on relationships. This is a storytelling model that seeks to deconstruct societal influences in conflict, and endeavours to create a more harmonious account of events.[10]

Policy-making mediation is a useful strategy for preventing conflict, problem-solving and ongoing conflict management in complex environments. It is a process whereby agreements reached at mediation are enacted in the development of policies, standards, procedures and regulations. Policy-making mediation is well suited to international conflicts that include issues of economic development and environmental and social sustainability.[11] It is appropriate for any area that requires policy development, including health, families, occupational health and safety, criminal justice, planning and the environment. Policy-making mediation is often used for developing environmental standards, as it is valuable for exploring the nature and causes of conflicts in the environment and identifying interests and priorities. It is useful for community consultations, as it facilitates the involvement of affected parties and others who are interested to express their views and participate in the policy-making process. Policy-making mediation is growing, as governments are increasingly restructuring legislation and regulatory procedures to include more conciliatory processes for conflict management.[12]

The model of mediation employed influences the manner in which the mediation is conducted. It also impacts upon the role assumed by the mediator and possible outcomes. The background, training and personal style of the mediator and the personalities of the parties involved influence the mediation model adopted. For instance, a mediator may have a stated preference for a particular model and apply this to every situation. Often, there are arguments over which model is superior to others. These arguments are in the main counterproductive. One model alone might work well if all conflict situations are the same. However, this is not the case and results in the limited application of one approach. The nature of the dispute will influence the choice of model, as well as external factors such as legal obligations, agency requirements and the availability of funds and other resources. Some agencies will only use a particular model of mediation and staff must undergo training in this approach, regardless of their pre-existing qualifications.

Different models of mediation exist and continue to be developed but they all share certain features. All of these models of mediation are underpinned by the win/win approach, except settlement mediation, which seeks a mid-point compromise.

Win/win

The win/win approach to conflict situations challenges the notion of compromise as a desired outcome by asserting that all parties to a conflict can be winners. This requires a shift in thinking as well as in terms of expectations. Rather than aiming for a mid-point compromise, the aim of win/win is to achieve as many goals as possible for all parties. This increases the positive expectations of what may be achieved. Although a win/win may not be possible in all situations, the parties will leave knowing that it has been attempted. A main principle underpinning the win/win approach is 'needs first, solutions later'.

In conflict management, people often endeavour to negotiate a mid-point that seems a fair compromise. Compromise may seem the simplest, easiest and fairest solution. It results in both parties having some of their needs met, with everyone at least sharing what is available. Compromise, however, often requires one party to give more and may cause resentment within the relationship. It has been described as an acceptable form of 'lose/lose' if both people lose an equal amount.[13]

While a mid-point may seem the fairest outcome, neither party achieves their desired outcomes. Compromise may result in a poorer quality solution than would result from a win/win approach. When deciding on options, the question is often asked, 'Is this a solution you can live with?' Again, this is not tackling the issue of whether or not it is in fact a desired outcome. Being able to 'live with' something is quite different from feeling as if you have won. It is interesting that the definition of mediation presented at the start of the chapter refers to 'an outcome that everyone can live with'.[14] But how can there be two winners? Generally speaking, if there is a winner, there is also a loser.

For a win/win to be achieved, it is necessary to

– separate the people from the problem

- focus on interests, not positions
- generate many options
- use objective standards to evaluate each option.

Two sisters go to the fruit bowl to get an orange but find there is only one left. What can they do to achieve a win/win solution?[15]
(Remember: needs first, solutions later.)

Mediation process

Mediation is generally divided into two phases. These are the problem-defining and problem-solving phases. Different stages and tasks are identified within each phase.

Phase one of problem-defining includes

stage 1: intake: determining appropriateness to mediate
stage 2: orientation
stage 3: storytelling
stage 4: identification of main issues: agenda setting.

Phase two of problem-solving includes

stage 5: developing options: mapping the conflict
stage 6: selecting options: negotiation and decision making
stage 7: agreement
stage 8: implementation and follow-up.

A separate meeting, referred to as private session, can be conducted at any time the mediator thinks appropriate. This is often held before stage 6: selecting options: negotiation and decision making, providing a reality check to evaluate levels of satisfaction with the mediation process, and to assess whether or not there is anything that may prevent the parties from entering into a negotiated agreement.

Different models of mediation emphasise particular stages or aspects of this fundamental model. For instance, narrative mediation focuses more on stage 3: storytelling of the mediation process.

Mediation practice

Mediation practice must be flexible to allow for difference, multiple perspectives and change. Assessment in mediation is about dialogue and providing a process of contextual interpretation that can lead to mutual understandings. Mediators allow for and expect contradictions, and multiple and changing interpretations. It is a search for shared understandings rather than absolute truth. Mediators frame problem categories in empowering language and identify main issues that allow for complexity and overlap. Well developed and effective communication skills are essential. These skills are the same as those used in counselling. However, it is the application of these skills that is different. In mediation, the focus is on conflict resolution and management for the future. The focus of counselling is personal change and development. However, the distinction is no longer so clear-cut, particularly in the newer transformative and narrative models of mediation.

Six core talents and skills of mediators are

- process management
- strategic intervention
- investigation
- presentation and discussion
- inventiveness, and
- empathy.[16]

Process management and strategic intervention are important throughout the entire mediation. Skills in assertiveness are also particularly important in the early stages to ensure that the parties have the opportunity to tell their stories uninterrupted and to be heard. Other skills and personal qualities that assist throughout the entire mediation are warmth, respect, humour, comfort and reassurance.

Investigation requires effective skills in listening and appropriate use of both open and closed questions. Paraphrasing is stating back to the person the content of what they have just said to you, using different language. This may seem a strange thing to do and may feel awkward during first attempts at using it. However, it is a useful skill for letting the person know you are listening and trying to understand what is happening. What better way than telling them what they have just said to you? The person will confirm or deny that you have understood correctly and then continue with further information. The choice of words, tone of voice and body language are important considerations. Parroting back exactly what the person has said is not helpful.

Summarising is also useful for letting the parties know you have listened and understood and can assist in providing a sense of order. Paraphrasing helps focus on the content and is useful for assisting parties to maintain control of their emotions. It is particularly useful in stage 3: storytelling. Focus is only on the content of what has been said and not on the emotions expressed. Feelings are dealt with in empathic responses, discussed in chapter 5, that respond to both feeling and content. Empathy is a particularly useful skill in stage 1: intake and in private session.

Presentation and discussion are important throughout the mediation and particularly so during stage 4: identification of main issues: agenda setting, when the mediator provides a summary of the stories presented in stage 3 and provides an assessment of the main issues in dispute. Inventiveness requires lateral and creative thinking by the mediator and the parties to come up with new solutions and is particularly important in stage 5: developing options: mapping the conflict.

Technology and e-mediation

Technology and in particular artificial intelligence have had major impacts locally and globally in the past three decades. In terms of mediation, we are generally considering technology as a tool to assist in the mediation process. However, it is important at the same time to consider artificial intelligence as a means of psychological manipulation with this discussed further in chapter 9 in the context of international peacekeeping.

Technology is now available across the many jurisdictions where mediation and other alternative dispute resolution approaches are used. This is in relation to the conduct of the mediation itself but also relates to the many processes and procedures that may occur before and following a mediation. This includes careful consideration of moral impacts related to confidentiality and privacy and communication between the parties outside of, and possibly during the mediation process.

Increasingly technology is being used for e-mediation, and particularly so since the introduction of Covid-19 social distancing restrictions. Mediators have had to consider whether to postpone mediations or to use virtual technologies. It is important to consider alternatives to mediation if this is not possible in person with flexibility, innovation and adaptability important during social distancing restrictions. Serious consideration is required of the complexity and jurisdiction of the dispute and what alternatives are available and preferred. This includes consideration of whether or not to delay the mediation. During Covid-19, legal aid in New South Wales has offered telephone mediation as a replacement for in-person mediation.

It is potentially difficult to conduct a complex mediation via technology. Ultimately, an electronic forum cannot replace an in-person mediation due to the lack of eye contact and difficulty reading facial expressions and body language. It is not possible to establish and maintain eye contact to develop trust and rapport, and to demonstrate listening and attentiveness when others are speaking which is so important during the early stages of a mediation and storytelling in particular. This difficulty in establishing eye contact is called 'parallax' and is caused by the displacement that occurs when a person is looking at the image of the speaker on screen and the camera is capturing this image as opposed to the person looking directly into the camera.

Unstable internet connections can result in a person being ejected from a mediation without notice, unclear or frozen images, distorted voices out of sync with the lips of the speaker, inability to have all cameras operating at the same time, with the possibility of distractions from crying children, barking dogs, nearby construction and ringing telephones and doorbells. If a party in an e-mediation is responsible for dependents, or other duties, it is not feasible to expect them to be able to fully participate. All of the parties might not attend the e-mediation with some saying they are available on call. They may join and not participate with their camera on, or turning it off and leaving or engaging in other activities. This may change throughout the mediation with the mediator struggling to maintain an effective process. Participants might use the excuse of poor technology, 'playing victim to technology', by pretending there are problems with connectivity or they lack the ability to actively participate.

Video conferencing does allow us to see facial expressions, upper body posture and to hear tone of voice. Preset backgrounds provide privacy for the person but can be surreal and distracting. Even when a virtual tour of the location is provided, people may be hiding off-screen, raising issues of privacy and confidentiality in terms of who is actually present and the possibility of the meeting being surreptitiously recorded. Showing our homes to people can expose social capital in the form of wealth, class and living arrangements. In video conferencing, we are looking at our own image and this might be distracting as well as highlighting differences such as age, gender, ethnicity, education, disfigurement and disability that may be more likely to produce stereotypes and anxiety when other aspects of communication are absent. A poor connection with background noise interference can make it harder to hear people and this can be exacerbated if a person has a strong accent or speech impediment. All of this can influence how powerful or powerless a participant feels and actually is in the process. The safety of individuals can be compromised if their home or work environment is exposed to other parties.

Email and text messages do not provide non-verbal social cues, unless a visual image or exclamation marks are included, and can reduce power differences. The mediator needs to be aware that parties may be texting each other during the e-mediation without the knowledge of the mediator and to include this in the ground rules. If a person has a low literacy and struggles with spelling, written communication is potentially embarrassing and disempowering for them. It is important the technology is suited to the goal of each stage of the mediation as well as being tailored to the distinctive features of the parties to balance power differences as much as possible. These asynchronous mediums are more likely to result in misunderstandings and possible escalation of the conflict. If communications become unclear, it is likely that a change in technology is required, and often this is a telephone call.

There are numerous benefits to online mediation including less effort in organising the mediation, and no time or costs for travel, and other costs including room hire. There are no geographical boundaries, with parties able to attend from any location in the world that has a secure internet connection. The goal of the communication and preferred communication styles will influence whether a synchronous or asynchronous technology is best suited. Asynchronous methods such as email and text can reduce emotional intensity and be preferred by acrimonious parties, including those with a history of violence, who do not want to be in the same room together, or the mediator has decided this is not possible due to safety reasons. These communications may be mediated through lawyers or advocates acting for each party and take the form of a shuttle e-mediation.

There are likely to be generational differences in preferred technologies and level of comfort for both the parties and the mediator. If parties prefer different mediums for communication, a balance that includes asynchronous and synchronous mediums to promote comfort and understanding is required. When using technology, a key consideration is to match the technology to the different stages of the mediation process.

For instance, first contact might be by telephone for introductory and intake purposes, followed by video conferencing to build rapport with email used to send documents for information sharing and text for negotiations. For video-conferencing, it is important that the mediator calls the meeting on a secure platform that is password-protected.

The mediator needs to ensure they have full control of the online administration to allow participants to enter the meeting, to ask them to exit the mediation, or to put them in different virtual rooms as required to ensure privacy and confidentiality, and to end the meeting and turn all microphones on or off.

Email and text communications can be at the convenience of the sender according to their own time zone. This can reduce power differences by removing visual signs of power and social interactions. Messages can be revised and well considered with input from others, and time to cool off overnight and review it the next day, if angry at the time of writing it. Text messages can be useful for brainstorming different options. Short and more frequent email and text message exchanges promote the flow of communication. The combination of regular texts and emails with strategic telephone calls can assist with reviewing progress to keep the mediation on track and to discuss details of final negotiations.

Ethical considerations and practice standards

Most mediators are working according to a professional code of ethics. These include the codes of ethics for social workers, lawyers, psychologists, planners and so on. These will relate generally to practice in your discipline area and in some situations also relate to specific areas of practice.

1. *What code of ethics is relevant to your work?*
2. *How familiar are you with this code? What aspects relate to mediation and conflict resolution?*

There is considerable debate about the desirability and feasibility of developing national standards for mediation and alternative dispute resolution. Regulation has come from the requirements embedded in legislation, employers' terms and conditions, and prerequisites for registration with different mediation and professional associations. In the absence of an over-arching professional association, complaints and discipline systems are also currently managed through these bodies. Mediation associations have varying prerequisites for membership. Professional associations, government departments and dispute resolution centres also have diverse preconditions for practice.

Codes of conduct require mediators to

- promote services accurately
- ensure effective participation by parties
- elicit information
- manage continuation or termination of the process
- exhibit lack of bias
- maintain impartiality
- maintain confidentiality
- ensure appropriate outcomes.[17]

How might you put each of these eight areas into practice?

Conclusion

Numerous models and approaches to mediation have been developed; a number of these models are detailed in this chapter. These include settlement, facilitative, evaluative and therapeutic mediation and the more recent mediation models of narrative, transformative, preventative and policy-making, as well as collaborative family law. The win/win approach endeavours to meet as many needs and concerns of all parties as possible rather than aiming for a mid-point compromise agreement that people are able to live with. The mutual gains approach provides a collaborative focus to negotiation whereby the parties share their needs, interests and concerns and information about possible alternatives in an effort to maximise gains for all parties. The type of dispute will inform the most appropriate mediation model. These different models share a similar process that is detailed in this chapter. This process is divided into the two phases of problem-defining and problem-solving; each phase comprises four stages. The approach of the mediator and application of this process will differ according to the mediation model used. Core talents and skills for mediators are identified, including process management and strategic intervention, investigation, presentation and discussion, inventiveness and empathy. Mediation practice is regulated by legislation, organisational contractual requirements and discipline-specific codes of ethics.

Relevant theories for mediation practice are discussed in the next chapter.

4

Theory and Mediation

For many mediators, the emphasis is on processes and skills alone; there is little evidence of use of theory, and this is reflected in training programs available. Lawyer and mediation educator from Bond University, Laurence Boulle, described mediation in the Australia in the early 1990s as 'a practice in search of theory'. He observed that while mediation had its foundations in several disciplinary areas, 'it has yet to develop its own explanatory theories'.[1] These main disciplinary areas referred to by Boulle were law, social work and psychology. Today these continue to be the main disciplinary groups practising in this area, with the addition of planning. A recommendation of the Attorney-General's Department on family mediation and issues of violence was that mediation training should include a substantial component on theory. The report stated,

> Training based on information and the understanding of the agencies' policies and procedures is not, on its own enough. Training should include a strong theoretical component so that all mediators understand the background to, and reasons for their actions.[2]

The criticisms of mediation in the 1990s are still relevant today, and many mediators rely predominantly upon models, processes and skills. In order to be effective workers in conflict management we need to have a view about what we are doing. Theory provides us with ways of looking at things from a range of different perspectives. It assists in developing models by describing principles and practices that have general application to conflict situations. Approaches to viewing and understanding conflict and human behaviour are provided, as well as explanations that assist in our understanding of actions and events. This can lead to prescriptions for actions in particular situations and contexts. By enabling you to describe and justify the choice and application of the particular conflict resolution processes and practices used, theory provides accountability to the people you are working with, yourself, managers, government and the general public.[3]

Some of the main theories and approaches relevant to mediation and conflict resolution are discussed in this chapter, including the theory of mutual gain. Social work critical theories are particularly relevant to this area of practice due to the focus on issues of power and social contextual factors. The critical theories discussed in this chapter include structural, feminist, anti-oppressive and anti-discriminatory, and postmodernism. Psychodynamic, lifestage and systems theories are also considered. The chapter concludes with a model for integrating theory and practice.

Conflict theories

Game theory

Game theory was created in 1946 by Jon von Neumann, a German mathematician, and Oskar Morganstern, a German economist, during their studies at Princeton University in the United States. It is a logical approach that involves mathematical modelling of social interactions between rational participants to develop games where individual benefits and losses are mathematically calculated according to the decisions made and actions of each person in the social interaction. Game theory has undergone further development and is applied across many disciplines and fields of practice, including social science, economics, international politics, biology, animal studies, environmental studies, psychology, sport, computing and armed conflicts. It is considered to be particularly suited to protracted conflict situations with high levels of conflict, hostility, violence and uncertainty. An early application of game theory of direct relevance to mediating conflict in criminal justice settings is the Prisoner's Dilemma, initially developed in 1950 by mathematicians Merril Flood and Melvin Dresher at RAND, a research and development organisation providing advice to the United States armed forces. This game demonstrates why two rational people may not co-operate even when it seems to be the preferred option. The game is as follows.

Two people are held separately in prison. The prosecutor does not have enough evidence to support the main charge but has sufficient information for a conviction of both of them on a less serious charge. At interview, each prisoner can (1) remain silent, (2) cooperate or (3) blame the other person. If both remain silent, they will both will be imprisoned for one year on the less serious charge. If one remains silent and the other does not, the person who remains silent will be sentenced to three years in prison and the other will be released. If they both blame each other, they will receive a prison sentence of two years.

The dilemma in this game is based on the principle that rational people are generally motivated by self-interest and will therefore choose an irrational option of non-cooperation over a rational choice that involves mutual cooperation even when mutual cooperation results in a superior outcome.[4]

Mutual gains theory

The mutual gains approach to negotiation underpins conciliatory approaches to conflict management, including alternative dispute resolution, restorative justice and therapeutic jurisprudence.

The theory of mutual gain, developed by Larry Susskind and colleagues (1996) in the United States in the mid-1990s is based on the premise that conflict can be prevented if parties to a potential dispute identify benefits to each party from reaching agreement. The concept of benefit also includes the prevention of loss. Mutual gain also presumes that self-interest can be identified with the interests of other parties or with a broadly defined common good. A mutual gains approach is useful for identifying main issues and considering the main needs and interests of different parties, and possible solutions that create value and are feasible. The mutual gains approach to negotiation is a four-stage process. These stages are

- preparation
- value creation
- value distribution
- follow-through.

Preparation requires critical analysis of other possibilities to a negotiated agreement to achieve best outcomes for all parties. The 'best alternative to a negotiated agreement' (BATNA) is a key concept underpinning the mutual gains approach. Parties weigh up both direct and indirect costs and benefits and consider ways of improving their own BATNA whilst raising questions about BATNA of other parties. After careful consideration of possibilities other than negotiated agreement, parties are better placed to decide whether it is in their best interests to stay or walk away from the negotiation process. Parties are then able to share their interests, needs and concerns in the knowledge that they can pursue their BATNA if the other parties are not responsive.

Value creation involves exploring the interests of all parties and generating a range of solutions to the problems raised. Brainstorming techniques are often used to generate a free flow of ideas and foster the development of creative responses. The preferred options are those that best meet the needs of most parties. The BATNA now provides a baseline for each party to assess the suitability of the options generated. It can be expected that how well each party's needs are met by the solutions generated will vary. Trading across differences provides a further opportunity for creating value. This assumes that parties will attach different values to the same things, with the differences becoming tradable commodities. Such differences include the value of time, money, goods and services and publicity, as well as expectations about the future that might include contingent responsibilities.

Value distribution aims to share the value created fairly among the parties involved in the negotiation process. Parties need to discuss and decide upon the development and application of objective measures to distribute generated value in a way that fosters positive ongoing relationships. These objective standards will take account of needs, abilities, precedents and measurable criteria. Building and maintaining trust in ongoing relationships creates an environment where the parties can engage comfortably and effectively in value creation and value distribution. This is important as the strength and durability of these relationships is crucial for successful implementation and follow-up.

Follow-through is concerned with the implementation of the negotiated agreement to ensure that the intended results are achieved. This involves agreement on the processes and procedures to be used for monitoring the implementation of the agreement. Responsibility for monitoring must be a mutual decision, with all parties confident that the processes will be abided by.

The mutual gains approach differs from traditional Western negotiation techniques, which are generally more adversarial and focused on maximising gains for one party only. In the mutual gains approach, the focus is on exploring the needs and interests of all parties; the maintenance and development of relationships are central. More traditional negotiation is often focused on solutions, with relationships secondary; each party generally determines what is wanted and makes demands above and beyond realistic expectations. Reasonable arguments put forward by the other party are discredited or undermined, with little or no empathy for their interests and concerns. Pressure is often exerted to obtain the desired results by forcing the other party to surrender to demands. Concessions might be given if the other side offers them first. The high levels of mistrust and aggressive behaviours damage relationships. It is difficult to trust someone who presents an inflated bottom line that is argued as non-negotiable, and then willingly accepts a lower offer.

Adversarial approaches are evident in Eastern cultures as well. The ancient Thirty-Six Strategems is familiar to most Chinese speakers.

These strategies apply to warfare, politics, business and daily life. Strategies include 'killing with a borrowed knife' to attack your adversary by using the strength of a third party, or better still to convince the third party to attack your enemy without your direct involvement. 'Hiding a dagger behind a smile' is a strategy to get close to your adversary for a surprise attack. Smiles are generally seen as friendly and can be disarming but can also be deadly when insincere. 'Fishing in muddied waters' means creating chaos and confusion so that the fish are easier to catch. This translates into the creation of division and discontent to cause confusion and fear. This is considered the optimal time to persuade others to become your ally and further your cause.[5] 'Wait at ease for the enemy' is a strategy to weaken the other person by tiring them through an active defence, rather than attacking them directly. Once their strength is reduced, the other side will have the upper hand. 'Make a feint to the east while attacking in the west' is a diversionary tactic with misleading or false information about intentions presented so that a surreptitious attack can be made in another area.[6]

Can you think of an example where one or more of these strategies was used? What was the result?

In reality, these adversarial approaches span all cultures and societies and are not restricted to either Western or Eastern cultures and are practices most of us are familiar with. It is important to be aware of adversarial strategies, and intervene if they are being employed in what is purported to be a conciliatory process.

A key component of a mutual gains approach is representation of diverse groups and interests and how the voices of minority groups are to be heard and included in the negotiation process.

Apply the mutual gains approach to the following scenario by either selling or purchasing a car.

Seller
Work has posted you overseas unexpectedly so you have decided to sell

your car. It is a Honda Accord. You purchased it for $35,000 less than 12 months ago. You approached the dealer to buy it back and were offered $20,000. You have decided to sell it yourself for an asking price of $27,000. You are quite desperate to sell as you leave for overseas in a fortnight.

Your advertisement reads,

'Honda Accord, black, plush interior, low kilometres, less than 12 months old. Excellent condition, 4 months registration, air conditioning, global positioning system and full stereo sound. Price: $27,000'

Buyer

You are after a new car and have looked at purchasing a brand-new Honda Accord. You have found the car that you like and have the money to go ahead and purchase it. It is a recent model, blue in colour, and will cost you $35,000. Your father has rung you to say that he has seen an advertisement for a similar car selling for $27,000. This seems like a good opportunity to save some money. However, you much prefer a blue car to a black one.

Critical theories

Critical theories used in social work provide a much-needed focus upon social and structural inequalities and the causes of oppression that are part of the social context within which all conflict occurs. Mediation has been criticised for its lack of focus on broader structural and social issues. Critical perspectives provide an analysis of power relationships in the conflict resolution process, particularly in terms of class, race, ethnicity and culture, gender, age, disability, spirituality and sexuality. Structural and feminist approaches contribute a focus on empowerment and social justice as well as addressing issues of access and equity for the most disadvantaged members of society.

Structural theory

The structural approach to social work practice was developed in the late 1970s and early 1980s and led by Maurice Moreau in the School of Social Work at Carleton University in Canada. Moreau (1979) asserted that traditional approaches to social work tended to place people in a dependent or passive position, with the focus of attention on the individual rather than their situation.

Structural social work was an attempt to move away from dichotomising the person and situation by focusing on interactions between people and specific social, economic and political circumstances. Power, both personal and political, is a main feature of structural theory. The focus of assessment is on a person's presenting problems and material conditions, and on dominant ideologies within a class structure. Ways in which the rich and powerful within society constrain and define the less powerful are of central concern to structural theory.

A major focus is concern for those who are less well off, who are obvious victims of economic inequality. Other groups, who may not experience economic hardship but who also suffer due to ideologies that support, legitimate or maintain the existing social order, are also of concern: how men define women, how heterosexuals define homosexuals, how white people define black and Indigenous people, how so-called normal people define those who are different, how adults define children and how the young define older people.[7]

The central goal of structural theory is to help people develop a social praxis. In other words, the aim is to assist the person to critically reflect on the personal, social, economic and political situation they are in by looking at who benefits and who suffers due to the labelling of behaviours, values, ideas or feelings as undesirable. The key task of a structural approach is to analyse how the dominant institutions define and interpret specific situations. For example, mediation and conflict resolution with women involves examining the connection between what are presented as personal problems, and a capitalist social structure that perpetuates the sexist, ideological and economic oppression of women.[8]

Analysis of the power relations between the person, worker and organisation is required. Is the relationship between the person and the worker, as organisational representative, one of service provision as a right or privilege, or is it mandatory that they attend? This is particularly relevant to mediation because increasingly what was a voluntary process is now mandated. Definitions of mediation in the early 1990s included the voluntary nature of mediation. However, mandatory use of mediation has come about with very little debate about implications for practice. Rather, mediators have embraced the increased demand for their services. Mediators and dispute resolution practitioners need to perceive, and understand, the contradictions inherent in their organisations and work. The next step is to strategically highlight and document these contradictions, and use them to advocate for change.

Structural theory focuses on the power dimensions in relationships. A dialogical relationship that does not involve the imposition of power by mediators over those they work with needs to be created. This is particularly challenging, and in some situations impossible, given the increase of mandatory mediation and the resultant enforcement of legislation, particularly in the areas of mental health and child protection. In situations of high levels of conflict, the worker may feel he or she needs to exert power over the parties to maintain an effective conflict resolution process. Workers must also be willing to give up positions of power and privilege. Self-awareness combined with political awareness is required, as well as awareness of ways in which we deal with power and powerlessness in our own daily lives and in our work as mediators.

1. *Is it reasonable to expect mediators to give up positions of power?*
2. *In what ways would this assist in the conflict resolution process?*
3. *In what ways might it be a hindrance?*

Feminist theory

Feminist theory developed in the 1980s and was based on the premise that people's material and emotional well-being can only be enhanced if gender is taken into account. This includes women's, men's and children's well-being. Gender-based inequality was viewed as 'permeating social relations in a profound way'.[9] Feminist theory rejects conservative determinism that regards women as subordinate to men due to nature. Also dismissed is the fatalistic view that gender issues are inextricably connected to class issues.

According to feminist theory, personal problems must be seen as political. Gender-related issues for women include violence, rape, incest, women's emotional welfare and women's work. Feminist interventions are therefore political in terms of identifying gender-based social problems, organising campaigns and networks and developing organisational structures to manage subsequent funding and resourcing of programs. Feminist theory questions the suitability of mediation in cases of violence and abuse towards women, arguing that mediation is privatising what should be a public concern. Feminist mediation and conflict resolution focuses on the expression and acknowledgement of women's emotions as legitimate, alongside activities to promote and develop self-confidence; women support each other in promoting anti-sexist practices for themselves as well as for other women.

Feminist theory identifies and confronts issues of gender inequality and discrimination in the workplace that impact upon female workers and women using their services. Feminist theory provides a dynamic perspective that places issues of inequality within a theoretical analysis of power, powerlessness and discrimination. The perspective has led to an increased knowledge and understanding of inequality and oppression and has attracted allegiance from other groups in the community who face oppression and discrimination.[10]

1. *Is it appropriate to mediate in situations where there is a known past history of violence from a male party towards a female party? Provide reasons for your answer.*
2. *Are there any contingency factors that might change your response?*

Jane is thirty-five years old and married with four children. She is employed as an academic and is required to teach and carry an administrative and coordination workload as well as complete a doctoral degree and publish in refereed journals. She finds she has no time left for writing once she has prepared her classes and completed coordination tasks. Jane's supervisor arranges a meeting with her to discuss lack of progress with her PhD and publications. Jane tells him her workload is too high and shares with him the family responsibilities she has outside of work hours. She argues that as a female she should be treated differently to her male colleagues who do not have the same family commitments that she has. Her supervisor argues that there is no difference between her and others employed at the same level regardless of gender.

1. *Should Jane be treated any differently to her male colleagues?*
2. *Is your response consistent with a feminist perspective?*

Anti-oppressive and anti-discriminatory theory

Anti-oppressive and anti-discriminatory theory originated in the United Kingdom in the late 1980s and was led by oppressed people who challenged the inadequacies of the prevailing system.[11]

The aim of anti-oppressive practice is social change directed at ameliorating social injustices.[12] A causal and interconnected relationship is seen to exist between discrimination and oppression. According to this analysis, it is necessary to deal with discrimination before oppression can be challenged. As with structural theory, this includes discrimination and oppression according to class, race, ethnicity and culture, gender, age, disability, spirituality and sexuality.[13] The theory focuses on the balance of power and whether or not a person who is facing discrimination in one or more areas can have their situation managed in a fair and equitable manner in mediation. For instance, in workplace mediation, a mature-age female factory worker with English as a second language may not have the sophistication of language of her male manager or confidence to represent herself adequately at mediation. Her situation may be complicated further by other areas of discrimination such as disability. An awareness of possible areas of discrimination assists the mediator to develop structures and processes to avoid the mediation process inadvertently being used to further oppress less powerful or disadvantaged individuals and groups in the community. Self-knowledge and the valuing of difference are central to engaging in anti-oppressive practices and challenging inequality.

Anti-oppressive practice challenges notions of professional power. It requires a strong alliance between service providers and service users to establish credibility. Empowerment can only be achieved through equal power relationships, and by professional relationships modelling anti-oppressive practices.[14] This is particularly relevant to debates led by the legal profession, about the professionalisation of the mediation and conflict resolution industry. Anti-oppressive and anti-discriminatory theory raises questions as to who is informing the debate and who will benefit from such changes. Serious concerns are raised if the answer is the professions themselves, and not those who are using their services. Further concerns are raised if the voices of service users are not listened to. The ideas expressed in anti-discriminatory and anti-oppressive theory have been further developed, particularly within critical postmodernism, and focus on issues of power, knowledge and difference.

Critical postmodernism

Critical postmodernism theory makes a valuable contribution to conflict resolution and mediation practice. It is difficult to begin a discussion of postmodernism without first considering modernism or 'modernity'. Modernity is the term used to describe what was regarded as rational, objective knowledge of the physical and social world. It had its origins in the early seventeenth century during a period that has now become known as the European Enlightenment. The disorder, superstition and cruelty of the Middle Ages was to be replaced by order, reason and universal knowledge. The application of reason to both the natural and social world saw the development of disciplines and professions such as physical sciences, medicine, economics and engineering. These professions have enabled new methods and means of capitalist production that have transformed countries worldwide. Through the development of grand theories, particularly of capitalism and socialism, modernism provided an emancipatory response to the negative effects of modernisation; namely disease, ignorance, poverty, and exploitation of people and of nature. The social sciences were regarded as crucial for this emancipation to occur. Expertise and professional responses were developed by the application of scientific knowledge of the social world, derived from the social sciences, to manage the social problems that were seen as an expected consequence of social change.

Postmodern critiques of modernism have focused on its claims about Western reason, universality and objectivity, as well as the totalitarian features. In contrast, postmodernism focuses on difference, emphasising the experiences of those who have been excluded from modernist critiques. Foucault criticises modernity for excluding the views of non-Europeans, women and members of lower socio-economic groups in general.[15] Much of postmodern writing reflects cynicism, disenchantment and despair with capitalism and modernist attempts to impose reason and order.

Postmodernism questions the intellectual integrity of modernity as a means for progress and freedom with modernism's grand theories embodying the dual forces of progress and oppression. Examples from throughout history are used to document the exploitation, cultural destruction, devastation, genocide and impoverishment that has occurred as a result of so-called progress under the guise of colonialism, imperialism and economic development.

The term 'meta-narratives' describes the grand theories that are used to legitimise the dominant social, political, economic and professional discourses. These include theories on racial purity, mental illness, the market economy, inferiority of women, the family and, more recently, globalisation and the new world order. These dominant beliefs have been incorporated into policies and professional practices such as psychiatric classification diagnostic systems and psychosocial models of family dysfunction.

Peter Leonard argues that the relationship between power and knowledge requires close attention focusing on the contradictions of emancipation and domination within modernism. He advocates for 'critical postmodernism' that rejects the self-interest and conservatism of postmodernism. Critical postmodernism requires engagement with service user groups and issues excluded by modernism including feminist, anti-racist and anti-colonial, environmental and socialist. Critical postmodernism questions the meta-narratives applied to issues of power and control, including assumptions about social justice, rationality and equality and new forms of power, particularly professionalism and cultural production. It opposes the view that global economic and cultural modernisation espoused by corporate capitalism will result in human progress. Engagement is with new concepts that are neither absolute nor relativist. It is through conversation, or discourse, that knowledge is developed. The result is interactive multiple views and realities that connect with and inform the broader political, economic and social structures.

Postmodern theory has made a major contribution to conflict resolution and mediation by focusing on such differences and acknowledging the legitimacy of different views and interpretations of the same event. It has particularly informed narrative, therapeutic and transformative mediation as the mediator listens carefully to each party's story and considers the social and contextual factors that have led to this interpretation of events, rather than simply trying to ascertain who is telling the truth and who is lying.

The technique of re-authoring is used to assist people to examine their stories from multiple perspectives focusing on issues of perceived or actual power and powerlessness that may have influenced the situation and behaviours of themselves and others at the time.

Bill, a psychiatrist, and Gayle, a community nurse, were employed on a psychiatric crisis response team. They were rostered on the afternoon shift together with several other staff. Bill and Gayle were to continue together on the night shift. The afternoon and night shifts required doing scheduled visits as well as responding to new calls.

Gayle was in her office on the telephone arranging a scheduled visit when Bill barged into her office unannounced and insisted she come with him as they had a crisis assessment to do. Gayle told him she already had another visit scheduled and asked if another staff member was available to do this visit with him.

Bill began shouting and swearing abuse at Gayle, calling her lazy and useless. While she was still seated, he physically stood over her and pressed his face close to hers. He then left the room and slammed the door behind him. Gayle followed, and saw him talking with another worker who was available to do the visit. Gayle was very upset and unnerved by this incident. She called her manager, who did not seem at all concerned. Gayle became worried about further work with Bill, particularly when they were rostered on alone at night together. She refused to return to work until the matter was dealt with, claiming she was fearful for her safety if alone with Bill.

A mediation session was arranged between Bill and Gayle. Bill denied that he raised his voice or abused or intimidated Gayle in any way. Rather than trying to ascertain who was telling the truth, the mediator proceeded to focus on Bill and Gayle's stories and different accounts of events. This was a validating experience for them both; new information and increased understandings were developed. The situation was discussed and stories re-authored in terms of power differentials including age, size, gender and professional status.

Bill was clearly older and more experienced than Gayle. He had a much larger and stronger physique and as a male psychiatrist believed that Gayle as a young and inexperienced nurse should follow his instructions. Gayle had the opportunity to tell Bill that she had another visit scheduled but would have willingly cancelled it if Bill could not find someone else to go with him. She also shared her feelings about how the incident had affected her. She spoke of the different nursing practices in the community as opposed to hospital wards and questioned the view of doctors being able to order nurses around. Bill listened to Gayle and apologised for his behaviour, promising to behave more respectfully in the future. They continued to work together amicably and no further incidents occurred.

Criminal justice theories

Criminal justice theories are important when considering different approaches to crime and punishment and how to management conflict associated with offending behaviours. This is within the context of burgeoning prison populations worldwide as well as increased interest in restorative justice approaches. These theories are relevant to different pathways and conflict management in the community as well as within often over crowded prison populations.

Desistance theory

Desistance from crime theory is particularly relevant to criminal justice and criminology concepts and approaches to crime prevention, sentencing, probation and re-entry and re-integration into the community.[16] It focuses on the interplay between personal factors, social structures and policy implications related to prevention, punishment, rehabilitation and community reintegration for offenders and ex-offenders.[17] The main aim is to stop recidivism. An early focus was on white males with more recent developments highlighting issues realted to gender, race and ethnicity and age (young people).[18] This is within the context of the Me Too and the Black Lives Matter movements in the early 2020s and in recognition of the over-representation of Indigenous peoples and young people in incarcerated populations worldwide. This follows the civil rights movements of the 1960s. Desistance from crime theory adopts an intersectionality approach to examine the inter-related systems of personal, social and political aspects of oppression and discrimination and the location of the person within this. For instance, a person may be experiencing longstanding inter-generational discrimination across a number of different domains while for others this has a far more recent onset such an acquired brain injury resulting from a sports injury or car accident. Some people will experience multiple levels of oppression due to ability, sexual orientation, gender, race and ethnicity, mental health, class, spirituality and so on. Others will not experience oppression or discrimination so it is important to consider the unique experience of each person in context.

Social recognition theory

Social recognition theory is a desistance theory that focuses on young people and different types of capital that they may or may not have access to. These forms of capital are social, economic, cultural and symbolic. Social capital includes positive and valued relationships, including peer groups and family that increase networks and access to resources. Economic capital is concerned with finances including income, assets and inheritance and paying taxes. This is essentials for daily life as well as luxuries or somewhere in-between such as having the ability to purchase a birthday gift for a child's friend when invited to a birthday party. Cultural capital incorporates social status, competence and reputation. It is about identity including a person's cultural identity, language and beliefs. This includes status derived from employment, knowledge and skill development and roles, networks and status in the community. Symbolic capital is the culmination of the recognition of social, economic and cultural capital and the benefits that flow from this recognition. It is essentially about self-esteem, social recognition and a person's reputation. This might be recognition of voluntary or paid contributions to the community to make reparation for past wrong doings or simply moving forwards and leading a good life as a contributing member of the community.

Transtheoretical approach: stages of change

The transtheoretical approach, developed by Proschaska and DiClemente, more commonly known as 'stages of change' is a core feature of desistance theory. It deals with concepts of ambivalence and motivation and is also known as 'motivational change'. Addressing ambivalence is seen as key to the desistance process with the aim of motivating the person to make positive choices and engage in a change process that supports healthy living. The main intervention arising from this theory, which is widely adopted in corrections settings and community substance misuse treatment services, is motivational interviewing. Motivational interviewing is underpinned by the five principles of: (1) empathy and effective listening that includes a non-judgemental approach; (2) assisting the person to develop an awareness of discrepancies in goals and current behaviours; (3) avoidance of arguments and the expression of oppositional views that could be seen as judgemental and labelling and result in defensive reactions; (4) go with the flow and avoid confronting or challenging resistance by inviting new perspectives without imposing these. This is in recognition that motivation to change and solutions will come from the person themselves and cannot be imposed by others; and (5) supporting autonomy and self-efficacy by demonstrating an attitude that is positive and hopeful and a belief that change is possible and the person is capable of making sound decisions for their future.[19]

Proschaska and DiClemente developed a six-stage cyclical model for behavioural change that has proven effective with substance misuse and chronic recidivism. These stages are (1) pre-contemplation when the person is not likely to be thinking about change; (2) contemplation when the person starts to think about the possibility of change; (3) preparation in terms of planning what to change and how to do so; (4) action taken to implement the plan; (5) maintenance to reinforce and sustain the changes and (6) relapse when the plan is abandoned and old behaviours re-emerge. It can often take several attempts for new behaviours to be fully established and is seen to be particularly helpful when working with long-term and entrenched behaviours.

Social learning theory

Social learning theory is considered core knowledge for understanding offending behaviours and underpins many prevention and intervention service models.[20] These service models include the Self Management and Recovery Training (SMART) program, originating from the United States, that is offered in both custodial and community settings as means of follow-up and transition. Two main SMART programs are Inside Out and Getting SMART. SMART is a peer-led voluntary program where peer support groups are used to facilitate the learning of new skills for a healthy life. Substance misuse is often identified as an area of need. The Good Lives Model combines learning theory and a strengths approach aimed at purposeful living that contributes to the community. A holistic approach is taken to the notion of a good life that includes inner peace, autonomy, happiness, friendship and creativity.[21]

According to social learning theory, crime is best explained as a learnt behaviour that is both direct and vicarious, and that develops in a social environment that favours and rewards criminal behaviours over law-abiding behaviours. More recent developments in social learning theory consider social learning alongside social structures examining group influences on individual behaviour particularly in relation to delinquency in adolescents. The socialisation process in families (of origin, surrogacy or choice) is interrogated in terms of parental role modelling, supervision and control over selection of friends. Key concepts are values, modelling and reinforcement. Peer effects are also a core and distinctive feature of social learning theory, with dominant peer behaviours found to have a strong influence on group attitudes and behaviours. According to social learning theory, if a young person is in a peer group where main interactions are associated with criminal behaviours they are more likely to adopt, maintain and escalate these attitudes and behaviours.[22] Learning theory recognises the interplay between biological and social theories and the dual effects of nature and nurture on criminal behaviours.[23]

Recent developments focus on self-directed autonomy and learning on how a person can influence a negative group subculture through positive role-modelling. This approach is now used to address substance misuse. In the past, an offender would be advised not to mix with friends and associates misusing substances and to find new friends. For most, this was not a realistic expectation, particularly post-release from prison. It is highly likely that a person will mix with established peers and networks, including drug dealers. This may or may not be initiated by the person themselves. Increased self-autonomy in decision-making and life direction and skills in assertiveness are targeted at making positive decisions, that may also influence peers, for a good life.

Deprivation theory

Deprivation theory examines the inter-relationship between economic inequality, disadvantage and offending. A key concept in deprivation theory is how individuals compare themselves and relate to a reference group of peers. Criminologists have a longstanding interest in the influences of 'relative' and 'absolute' deprivation on crime. Relative deprivation as the name implies is relative to the circumstances of others and this is generally a comparison with those who consider themselves to have less than their peers, experiencing frustration, anger, resentment and a sense of entitlement. This is characterised by a cognitive process that begins with a comparison of circumstances, followed by an appraisal of disadvantage perceived to be unfair, and ultimately resulting in resentment.[24] Ultimately, it is about subjective responses to an objective reality. Deprivation can be experienced across a range of situations including access to the basics of: food and water, clothing, housing, energy resources, healthcare, education, adequate income, education and employment. It is not simply that these basics are provided; it is important that they are perceived to be adequate, appropriate and affordable for a reasonable quality of life.

The last five decades have seen an increased focus on absolute deprivation, and structural economic disadvantage has ben found to be a strong predictor of violent crime in the United States.[25] Deprivation theory has also been used to increase knowledge and understanding of the experience of different prisoner population groups. Women prisoners have been found to experience higher rates, and increased severity, of mental health issues related to anxiety, depression and trauma and suicidal ideation when compared to women in the community. Contributing environmental stressors are from incarceration, isolation, separation from family and friends, and treatment by staff and other prisoners. This highlights the need for closer attention to the conditions of confinement of women prisoners that ultimately effects their re-integration back into the community.[26]

Importation theory

Importation theory is concerned with difficult behaviours brought into custodial environments. This theory is underpinned by the premise that disciplinary issues and misconduct in prisons arise from negative attitudes, beliefs and behaviours that people bring with them into the prison environment. This can result in violent subcultures in the community replicating these power structures in the prison environment. Importation variables considered include age, gender, race and ethnicity, cultural belief systems, marital status, education, employment, substance use, prior offending and incarceration, history of violence and gang membership.[27]

Importation theory is generally considered to be more useful in predicting more serious crimes and infractions of aggressive and antisocial behaviours. Studies have been predominantly of male offenders, and associations have been found between prior violent offending and serious prison infractions with violent behaviour in prison a predictor of violence in the community post-release and recidivism.[28] Far less is known of importation factors and female prisoners, with a recent study finding that importation factors associated with higher levels of reported prison misconduct were prior trauma, homelessness, financial difficulties, victimisation and self-harming behaviours.[29]

Difficult and antisocial behaviours can also be deported to health settings when offenders are ordered for a psychiatric assessment at psychiatric units in general hospitals in the community. This includes people who have been arrested in the community for offending or people on prison transfer. This has resulted in behaviours such as spitting fights and the throwing of heavy objects now being observed in general hospital psychiatric units amongst these patients. This is within the context of vulnerable people from the general community who may be admitted for anxiety, depression, trauma, schizophrenia, a mood disorder or eating disorder. This raises the question of where offenders should be imported to for psychiatric assessments and whether or not it is appropriate to use general hospital acute psychiatric units for this purpose.

Theories on personal development and life stages can provide insights into communication in conflict. It is worth noting that these theories are rejected by some critical theorists as being too positivist and restrictive. However, it is argued that if they are applied liberally, they can provide valuable insights into people's behaviours and needs at different ages and stages of their lives.

Psychodynamic theory

A focus of psychodynamic theory is on personality and interpersonal relationships. Emphasis is on developmental stages, personality development and unconscious processes. Eric Erikson developed a model of personality development linked with biological development. According to this model, psychological and physical development are linked with identifiable stages of physical development and associated psychological tasks at each stage. Erikson's stages of psychosocial development and developmental tasks are presented in figure 4.1.

Figure 4.1

Erikson's stages of psychosocial development and developmental tasks

Stage	Task
Early infancy – birth to 1 year	Trust vs mistrust
Later infancy – 1 to 3 years	Autonomy vs shame and doubt
Early childhood – 4 to 5 years	Initiative vs guilt
Later childhood – 6 to 11 years	Industry vs inferiority
Puberty and adolescence – 12 to 20 years	Ego identity vs role confusion
Early adulthood – 21 to 40 years	Intimacy vs isolation
Middle adulthood – 41 to 60 years	Productivity vs stagnation
Late adulthood – 61 years and over	Ego integrity vs despair

The ages specified by Erikson for each developmental stage are an approximate guide and allow for wide variation according to individual differences; each of the stages overlaps. Goals are identified for each stage of development but Erikson's model recognises that these may be completed at a different stage in a person's life.

In early infancy, from birth to approximately twelve months, trust is established, with caring adults demonstrating love and responding to the baby's needs. In turn, the baby learns to trust and love others.

During later infancy, approximately one to three years of age, the child becomes more autonomous while also conforming to rules and routines.

At approximately four to five years of age, early childhood, the child demonstrates increased initiative and exploration of her or his environment. Fantasy and role play of adult activity occurs; the child often copies the parent of the same sex and adopts similar behaviours and attitudes. Positive self-esteem develops by engaging in new tasks and receiving positive feedback from significant others.

Later childhood, around six to eleven years, is characterised by industry and accomplishment; the child has seemingly boundless energy. During this stage, the child learns new intellectual, practical and social skills. The child is to be encouraged to participate in a range of group activities and interests, and to learn skills in cooperating with others and competing in appropriate ways. The child's self-esteem develops through the positive feedback received from her or his efforts and accomplishments.

During puberty and adolescence, from approximately twelve to nineteen years, major changes are occurring physically and emotionally, with increased sexual feelings and attractions. This period is distinguished by a desire for increased independence often associated with feelings of self-doubt and confusion. Association and identification with peers takes on increased importance; parents' standards are temporarily rejected. This is seen as necessary for the development of an independent identity.

In early adulthood, between the approximate ages of 20 and 40 years, the main developmental task is intimacy. This requires trust and commitment between two people. In a sexual relationship, this is characterised by love, concern and compassion. Intimacy is also a feature of long-standing friendships. Those who do not relate with others on an intimate level can be seen as aloof and unfriendly and can have difficulty establishing relationships.

The main task of middle adulthood, between forty-one and sixty years of age, is productivity and giving back to others. This may be in relation to children and grandchildren, mentoring younger colleagues or community action and involvement. Those who do not successfully achieve this stage can be seen to be self-interested and preoccupied with their own needs to the exclusion of others.

Erikson's final stage is late adulthood for those aged over sixty years. Integrity is the main developmental task and living with dignity. This requires having a sense of meaning and purpose in life as well as order. Integrity results in joy for living in contrast to despair that can develop in older people due to unresolved issues of loss and grief.

Abraham Maslow, a founding humanist psychologist, developed a hierarchy of human needs that must be met for a person to achieve psychological maturity. Maslow's hierarchy of human needs in order of attainment is

- physiological needs
- safety needs
- love and belonging needs
- esteem needs
- self-actualisation needs.

Physiological needs include food, water, oxygen, clothing and shelter, sleep and excretion. Safety needs comprise predictability and reliability in physical, psychological and social arrangements. The need to love and be loved and to have a sense of belonging and emotional security is important for the development of trust and intimacy. Self-esteem is about having a positive self-image. This develops from feelings of love and acceptance from significant others. It involves feeling competent and having a good reputation. Self-actualisation needs are concerned with achieving one's full potential.

For Maslow, it was necessary to successfully attain each level before moving to the next. This may be relevant for basic physiological needs for survival, but the other needs are not necessarily met in a chronological order. In many ways, Maslow's hierarchy of needs is an ideal typology achieved by very few. There is a temptation for workers to unwittingly judge and pathologise a person according to whether or not they have passed a particular stage. However, if it is applied more liberally, Maslow's hierarchy acknowledges the complexity of people's lives, including strengths as well as areas of need.

Life stage theories

Theories on the life cycle focus on the family, with six main life stages identifed. Life cycle theories have been criticised for not fully recognising the range of different life trajectories; not all people follow these stages. However, it is worth considering some of the tasks identified for each life stage and whether or not they apply to the people you are working with, particularly families.

Stage 1 'unattached young adult' focuses on increasing independence from the family by defining clear boundaries and becoming more autonomous. Intimate relationships are also developed.

Stage 2 'couple': the emphasis is on working out new roles and new loyalties and setting boundaries with partner, family and friends. This includes reconciling two sets of myths or traditions about sex, parenting and behaviour.

Stage 3 'birth of children': the power balance changes as parenting roles are negotiated and defined. Who decides what is a central consideration as well as children's power. The first child requires acknowledgement and decisions based on two sets of family traditions. This is more complex in cross-cultural relationships or where religious beliefs differ.

Stage 4 'bonding with first child, subsequent children' requires renegotiating relationships with grandparents and establishing new boundaries between parents and children. New alliances are formed, particularly when children commence school.

Stage 5 'family with adolescents': parents renegotiate their relationship and prepare for death of grandparents. Power starts to shift from parents to children; space and privacy lead to autonomy. This stage sees the launching of children, loosening of boundaries and the empty nest. This stage has become delayed for many families with children now staying at home for much longer periods, primarily due to economic reasons. In situations of separation and divorce, new boundaries and expectations of parents and children are required. This involves grief and loss for children and partners and renegotiated parenting roles. Although marriage stops, parenting continues. Issues arise over maintenance of contact with grandparents and other relatives and loyalties for parents and children. To compensate for the roles performed by the absent parent, children may be given inappropriate tasks for their age. Lifestyle changes and a redefinition of self occurs for the separating couple. 'Remarriage or re-coupling' involves coming to terms with the previous marriage or relationship and the different stages of development for each family where there is often no shared history. Where families have known each other previously, relationships, including parenting, need to be renegotiated. Adjustments to the extension of family are required. For instance, this may now include four or more sets of grandparents.

Stage 6 'family in later life' focuses on the role of grandparents, retirement and loss of status and dealing with one's own death. It is seen as a time of integration where new generations are supported while at the same time the older person needs to be supported, particularly if they are ill or dependent.[30]

The application of a critical theoretical lens to generational comparisons identifies social, political and economic contextual factors that influence development and behaviour.

Systems theory and eco-maps

In the 1960s, systems and ecological perspectives were used in family therapy as a way of conceptualising relationships. The focus was on principles of complex, adaptive systems that were continually changing, and generating new patterns of actions, interactions and meanings.

Explicit assumptions were that people have a right to control their own lives and that society has an obligation to ensure that people have access to resources, services and opportunities that they need to meet various life tasks, to alleviate distress and realise their values and aspirations. When providing services, the dignity and individuality of the person must be respected, with interventions maximising participation of parties and self-determination. Social problems and conflict were viewed as manifestations of a breakdown in the interactions between people and their environments.[31]

Key concepts in a systems approach were 'interaction' and 'problems in living'. Interaction was seen as dynamic and constantly changing, with a focus on the interconnectedness and interdependence between the person and her or his 'whole' environment and adaptation or 'goodness of fit'. The emphasis of 'problems in living' was on life transitions, environmental pressures and interpersonal processes. The aim of interventions was to achieve a balance or 'steady state' that alleviated tensions and provided stability. In true modernist form, this steady state was also referred to as 'homeostasis' and was likened to the thermostat on a heater. Many of the concepts and examples used were from engineering and the physical sciences.

Difficulties were seen as having a variety of causes with multiple ways of achieving goals. The family was divided into marital, parental and sibling sub-systems. A focus was on boundaries and transactional patterns between these three subsystems. The idea of reciprocity was important in that if change occurs in one subsystem, change is likely to occur in another as a flow-on effect. Genograms were used to plot the family tree on both sides, preferably across three generations. Ecomaps were used as a tool to chart social connections and their quality.

Early writings on systems and ecological perspectives were generally from a white middle-class perspective in language that today is considered disrespectful and disempowering.[32] Families were described as 'dysfunctional'; mothers were often blamed for being too 'enmeshed' or 'disengaged' and held responsible for family problems. Family therapy has evolved to focus more on family strengths and this is reflected in more positive non-judgemental language. A focus remains on the family system with a much greater emphasis on the quality of attachments. This has come to be known as attachment based family therapy.

A main contribution of systems theory to conflict management is the mapping of relationships and social environment in stage 5 of the mediation process: developing options: mapping the conflict, discussed in more detail in chapter 6 on problem-solving. Systems theory is particularly useful when mediating family, parent adolescent and adult–elder conflicts due the emphasis on interactions and the quality of attachments.

Integrating theory and practice

Many workers find it difficult to establish meaningful links between theory and practice or to acknowledge the important contribution of theoretical frameworks in their practice. Therefore, it is not surprising that making these connections between theory and practice presents as a major challenge for students. How do we then integrate theory and practice? To make the necessary connections between theory and practice, we need to give it operational meaning. Marion Bogo and Elaine Vayda have adapted the work of Kolb on experiential learning to social work education and developed what they call the 'integration of theory and practice loop' (ITP loop).[33] This has been further developed by Martin, McKay and Hawkins as the 'theory and practice spiral' and is applied more broadly to the human services, including conflict resolution and mediation. The theory and practice spiral is presented on the next page in Figure 4.2.[34]

The theory and practice spiral can be applied to a wide variety of conflict situations, including those with a small number of parties as well as complex multiparty disputes.

In applying the theory and practice spiral first, the factual elements of a conflict situation are retrieved. Second, reflection focuses on assumptions about power and what works for and against empowering practice. The mediator identifies personal assumptions, attitudes and values that may impinge upon the conflict situation. For instance, class, cultural and gender assumptions and biases must be identified in order to understand and attempt to manage their power and influence. Crit-

Figure 4.2

Theory and practice spiral

REFLECTION

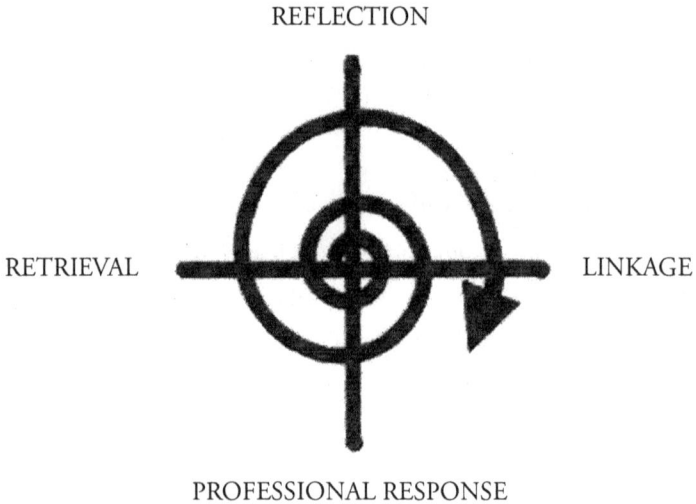

RETRIEVAL   LINKAGE

PROFESSIONAL RESPONSE

ical reflection guards against 'unwitting' disempowering practices.[35] Third, linkages are made with theory that can account for or explain the information retrieved and personal reflections on this. This in turn leads to an informed professional response. This process continues as new information is retrieved. Following is an example of the application of the theory and practice spiral.

Retrieval

The police referred a dispute between two neighbours for mediation. They had responded to a call from an eighty-three-year-old man Max, who had called them to complain that his neighbour Jean, sixty years of age, had threatened and yelled abuse at him and thrown his pot plants over the second floor balcony, smashing them on the ground. He was very upset and agitated when he rang the police and said he was fearful that Jean would attack him.

The worker agreed to mediate between Max and Jean. The police provided the addresses and telephone number for Jean. Max did not have a telephone. Unable to reach Jean by phone, the worker went directly to the public housing apartments and knocked on her door. The mediator observed a number of neighbours watching as she waited for Jean to answer.

When Jean answered the door, the worker said, 'Hello, are you Jean?'

Jean, looking agitated and dishevelled, retorted, 'And who wants to know?'

The worker informed Jean that she was a mediator at the local neighbourhood dispute centre and that she had received a referral from the police about her being abusive towards her neighbour Max and throwing his pot plants over the balcony.

Jean looked as if she might explode and shouted, 'Lies. It's all lies. He tried to poison me. Nobody's worried about me, are they? Lock him up. Lock him up.'

The mediator asked, 'Can I come in to talk about this?' but Jean slammed the door in her face.

Reflection

The mediator was encouraged by her supervisor to reflect on the effect her unannounced arrival may have had on Jean. She also speculated on whether the neighbours had heard what had been said about the incident with Max and what effect this may have had. The mediator also realised that as she waited for the door to open, she became more and more uncomfortable. Her supervisor suggested that she try to re-experience that uncomfortable feeling and speculate on its source. The mediator was able to talk about her discomfort at having to confront Jean with the details of the referral from the police when she really wanted to establish a trusting relationship with her and endeavour to assist her and Max to resolve their differences.

Linkage

The mediator was struggling with the role of authority vested in her by the police and the apparent contradiction with critical theories that focus on care and control and power. The supervisor identified the mediator's conflict in these terms and helped her to seek a way to reconcile the contradiction. This might be achieved by looking for the positive aspects of authority as a means to engage that part of Jean's desire to live peacefully and believe she is being cared for and protected in the process. This could be achieved by providing more introductory information as well as reframing the content of the referral in neutral and non-blaming language. A more engaging statement might have been as follows.

'Hello, I'm (name), a mediator from the Neighbourhood Mediation Centre. The police have asked me to come and check that you're safe and that everything's okay. Do you mind if I come in for a chat?'

Structural theory and anti-oppressive and anti-discriminatory theories provide an analysis of discrimination and oppression according to class, race, ethnicity and culture, gender, age, disability, spirituality and sexuality. The age difference was significant as Max was nearly twenty years older than Jean and he was quite frail. He was unsteady on his feet and worried that if Jean pushed him, he might easily fall. Max's accent was difficult to understand. Jean made it clear she did not like in her words 'foreigners'. Jean had recently moved in to her apartment and was not sleeping well. Both Jean and Max were quite socially isolated and had few visitors or friends.

The intake assessment revealed that Jean had a diagnosis of bipolar-affective disorder. The stress of the move, social isolation and other factors had resulted in her mood becoming quite elevated in recent days. Jean was reluctant to talk about this and did not want her neighbours to know she had a mental illness. She wanted a fresh start. Jean was a Christian; her religious beliefs provided comfort and hope.

Anti-oppressive and anti-discriminatory theory alerted the mediator to the discrimination and oppression that Jean may have experienced because of her mental illness and how she needed to be sensitive and thoughtful in her approach to this. It also alerted her to other areas of discrimination they both experienced due to class and Max due to his cultural background. Feminist theory also highlighted the lost opportunities and discrimination Jean faced as a woman throughout her life.

Postmodern theory reminded the mediator of the importance of listening carefully and validating both Jean and Max's stories, and to re-author them in a manner that would foster mutual understandings and more neighbourly relations between them.

Professional response

The mutual gains approach was useful to identify the main issues and consider the needs, interests and concerns of Jean and Max so that viable solutions leading to improvements for both of them could be implemented. By adopting a win/win approach, the mediator endeavoured to address as many needs and concerns of both parties as possible. Preparation required critical analysis of other possibilities to a negotiated agreement for them both in terms of best possible outcomes. Both wanted to stay living in their public housing apartments, neither having a better alternative. The worst alternative for both of them was to have to struggle in private rental accommodation. Shuttle mediation was used due to the level of tension between the two of them. Value creation involved exploring the interests of both Max and Jean; brainstorming was used to generate a range of solutions to the problems raised. A main solution reached by Jean was that she needed to remain as mentally well as possible if she was to maintain a reasonable quality of life in her new apartment. She agreed to see her psychiatrist, who arranged for a brief hospital admission to settle her disturbed sleep and mental state, to reduce her irritability and thereby lessen the likelihood of further conflict between herself and Max. Max and Jean developed increased understanding, empathy and care for each other in the mediation process, and they become good neighbours and friends; Max was Jean's only visitor during her brief hospital admission.

Conclusion

The main contribution of social work critical theories – structural, feminist, anti-oppressive and anti-discriminatory, and postmodern theory – is giving emphasis to social justice and ensuring that people are not knowingly or unwittingly discriminated against in the mediation process. Of central concern are ways in which the rich and powerful within society constrain and define the less powerful. Sources of possible discrimination and oppression are class, gender, race, ethnicity, and culture disability, age, sexual preference and spiritual beliefs. Feminist theory stresses the importance of issues of gender inequality and the connection between the personal and political. The focus on issues of inequality and developing anti-discriminatory and anti-oppressive practices, has further enriched practices in conflict management and mediation. Critical postmodernism calls upon mediators to critically examine the relationship between power and knowledge and the dominant discourses used in mediation practice. When applied liberally, psychodynamic and life stage theories can provide valuable insights into people's behaviours and needs at different times of their lives with systems theory useful for mapping the conflict. The theory and practice spiral provides a useful model for integrating personal reflections, theory and practice. The following two chapters take a closer look at the problem-defining and problem-solving phases of the mediation process.

5

Problem Defining

Mediation is generally divided into the two phases of problem defining and problem solving.[1] The stages in the problem-defining phase of mediation are discussed in this chapter. These include intake, orientation, storytelling and identification of main issues.

Mediation stage 1: intake: determining appropriateness to mediate

Not all conflict or potential conflict situations are suitable for mediation. The starting point therefore is to determine appropriateness to mediate by considering the following questions:

1. Are the risks too great, or uncertain, for parties to be able to negotiate effectively?
2. Are external contingencies such as existing laws, rules and procedures going to prohibit a fair and equitable outcome?
3. Can the uncertainty of the future be adequately predicted for negotiation and agreement preparation in the present to be effective?[2]

General considerations at this stage include defining the parameters of the problem, identification of external constraints, and establishment of a conflict management goal that includes information exchange and the identification of issues and interests. Deciding who should participate, and in what role, is a crucial part of preparation to mediate.[3]

Mediation stage 2: orientation

If mediation is deemed a suitable process, and a commitment to participate is obtained from all parties, the next step is the establishment of the process, and rules of engagement. For the mediation to be effective, it is important that the process and rules are accepted as appropriate by the parties involved. These will vary according to context and the different cultural rules and norms that operate. The mediation rules aim to ensure an orderly process that is fair and equitable to all participants. Some basic rules and principles are that the mediator be neutral, unbiased and fair and that each person in turn has the opportunity to speak without interruptions.4 Of prime importance is the establishment of a clear and transparent process that allows participants the opportunity to effectively state their concerns and to be involved in the identification of main issues and in effective negotiation. The mediator's role is to ensure effective participation by parties, to elicit information, to manage continuation or termination of the process, to demonstrate lack of bias, to be impartial and to ensure appropriate outcomes.

When deciding upon the location and set up of the venue in which the mediation session is to occur, careful consideration of issues of power is needed. For instance, in a workplace mediation between a supervisor and supervisee, it is not appropriate to have the session conducted in the supervisor's office – even though this may be suggested by management. Seating of parties is also important both when waiting to attend the session, as well as in the room where the session will be held. Possible intimidation is a crucial consideration.

Breanna made an application to sue her builder only to find she was required to attend a compulsory mediation session. She decided to attend the session in good faith and, while not expecting a satisfactory resolution, was hopeful. She was not looking forward to being in the same room as the builder because in past dealings he had been abusive and threatening toward her.

To Breanna's surprise, when she attended the mediation session, there were two men in suits present, neither of whom she recognised. The mediator sat at the end of a rectangular table and placed Breanna directly opposite the two men, who turned out to be a company representative and a barrister. The mediator simply said at the start, 'We'll stay here for as long as it takes.'

The barrister began employing adversarial techniques by putting Breanna down, shaking his head when she spoke and staring at her continuously during the session.

Breanna felt his staring was deliberate intimidation and eventually said, 'I don't have to put up with this.'

The mediator immediately called for a private session with Breanna and asked the other parties to leave the room. She said to Breanna, 'If you're finding this difficult, imagine how you'll be if this goes to court and you're put in the witness box. The case could go on for a week or more. This is nothing compared to that.'

Breanna was horrified by this response from the mediator, who she believed had interpreted her legitimate concern as a sign of weakness rather than as the bullying tactics of the other side. She lost faith in the process and the ability of the mediator to understand her situation at all.

Not surprisingly, this matter was not resolved.

At the end of the session, the mediator asked for feedback from Breanna, 'How was I?' she asked, with a big smile on her face.

Breanna was surprised at the question and by this time had a splitting headache. 'How should I respond?' she wondered. Her response was influenced by what she saw as the total insensitivity of the mediator to her needs and concerns and the futility in trying to once again get her to understand her situation. Breanna also wanted to get out of there as quickly as she could. However, she did not want to get the mediator offside as she feared damaging her case in some way. The session had lasted for three hours without any breaks. Breanna forced a smile and said, 'You were fine,' and then left.

1. *What might be a more suitable seating configuration?*
2. *Should the parties be informed of who will be at the mediation session?*
3. *Should they have a say at all in who attends and in what capacity?*
4. *How might the mediator have handled Breanna's complaint in a way that would have had a positive effect on the mediation process and outcome?*

At the start of the session, the mediator is the focus of attention, and each party is able to see the others without being in direct eye contact. Seating is often in a semicircular arrangement at this stage, with the mediator at the front. As the process continues, seating configurations will change in accordance with the particular stage of the mediation. For instance, in phase 2 of the mediation, where negotiations are occurring, the parties will be sitting face to face as they will be talking directly to each other at this time.

The mediator introduces all parties and outlines the process to be followed in an opening statement. The aim of the opening statement is to establish the credibility of the mediator, the ground rules, and the purpose and procedures of the session. Topics covered include the voluntary or involuntary nature of the mediation, the mediation process to be followed, confidentiality, the credibility and neutrality of the mediator, and informing participants that decisions in mediation are future-focused and are not legally binding.

1. *What personal qualities would you look for in a mediator?*
2. *Prepare an opening statement. Write this statement down and then practise reading it to someone else as if you are really opening up a mediation session.*
3. *Get feedback about the content of the statement as well as the manner in which it was delivered.*
4. *Repeat this exercise, with the other person now delivering her or his statement and you providing the feedback.*
5. *Would you like to be a party in a 'real' mediation conducted by this person? If yes, why? If not, why not?*

Private session

Like stage 1: intake, the private session occurs (as the name suggests) with each party alone. Where there are two mediators, they usually see both parties together, rather than seeing a party each. In the short term, this is more time-consuming and costly, but it avoids splitting between the mediators, and ultimately, if the mediation is successful, it reduces time and costs. Private session can be conducted at any time the mediator thinks appropriate, as illustrated in the example of Breanna. Sometimes mediators use a model where private session is a distinct stage in the mediation process. It is added as an additional stage in between stage 5: developing options and stage 6: selecting options. However, private session is included here as it may be included in phase 1 if judged necessary by the mediator.

A separate session conducted with each party provides an opportunity to reveal any concerns they may have that they do not want to disclose in a joint session. A separate session may be introduced at any time in the proceedings, at the discretion of the mediator. The main purpose is to enable the parties to raise issues that may hinder effective negotiations. It is also a chance for the mediators to empathise with each party to develop trust in the mediator and the process.

In conflict in interpersonal relationships, screening for violence is an important feature of the private session.[5] It cannot be assumed that the intake assessment will remain the same for the duration of the mediation, particularly in situations where there is a known history of violence or aggression. After the private meetings, both parties are brought back together to engage in further discussions. Or, if they have reached the negotiation stage, they can commence bargaining directly with each other to work out the details of the agreement.

If an agreement to resolve the dispute has not been reached, the mediator will reassess the process and may move back to an earlier mediation stage. For instance, one party may be still feeling very angry and not ready to move on. This may be a signal that more time was needed for stage 3: storytelling to let that person tell their story, or more time in private session to let them express their feelings and have them acknowledged.

It may be necessary to refer a party for counselling to be conducted alongside the mediation process or to delay the mediation process until all parties are ready. If ultimately the parties are still not in agreement, as in the case of Breanna and the builder, the mediator will endeavour to reach an agreement on alternative ways of dealing with the dispute. Particularly in situations of mandatory mediation ordered by the courts, the next step may already be predetermined.

What is known as 'shuttle mediation' occurs when the parties are located in separate rooms or locations and the mediators conduct the mediation through a series of private sessions. Shuttle mediation is generally used where it is deemed unsafe or unsuitable for the parties to be in the same room together. Extra time needs to be allowed for conducting shuttle mediations. There may be stages in a regular mediation when the mediator reverts to a shuttle mediation process. This may occur at the negotiation stage, offers being taken back and forth by the mediator. This is what the mediator did with Breanna and the builder. Rather than assisting them to conduct their own negotiations together, she kept them in separate rooms and went back and forth with offers and counter-offers. In their review of mediation practice in the Supreme and County Courts of Victoria in Australia, Sourdin and Balvin (2009) found a tendency for mediators to use shuttle mediation following introductions and questioned whether or not this process was actually mediation.

Empathy

As mentioned in chapter 3, empathy is a particularly useful skill in private session. Private session provides an opportunity to check with parties about how the process is working for them and whether there are any issues or concerns that may impede the mediation process. It is also an opportunity for the mediator to further develop a good working relationship with each party separately acknowledging their feelings..

Many of the skills used in conflict management are skills we use in everyday conversation, such as eye contact, listening, and open and closed questions. There are also skills that are not commonly used in everyday contexts but are used more in counselling and conflict management. Empathy is one of these. Learning new skills such as empathy can seem awkward but the more you practise the the easier it becomes. This is like learning any new skill. If a skill is new or more complex, you often don't get it right the first time.

It is easy to reject as unnecessary skills that are unfamiliar or to argue that a simulation is not the same as a real mediation. It is easy to say you already know how to do it. If that is the case, practise it to become even better by modifying the model below and in your own language.

There are many reasons for becoming good at empathy. Empathy conveys respect. It is an unobtrusive means of helping people explore themselves and their problem situations. If people feel understood, this influences them to continue on and explore a situation more widely or more deeply. Empathy encourages and facilitates communication. It can play an important part in establishing rapport with a person. Since it is a way of staying in touch with people and their feelings and experiences and behaviours, it can provide support throughout the entire mediation process.

Empathy involves listening carefully to the other person and then communicating understanding of what the person is feeling and of the experiences and behaviours underlying those feelings.[6] Empathy is used in private session and sometimes during intake. It is the mediator's way of saying, 'I'm with you, I've been listening carefully to what you are saying as well as your feelings about it and I'm checking to see if my understanding is accurate.'

There is a difference between a person talking about feelings and emotions that took place during the conflict, and their expression of feelings and emotions during the mediation. Both need to be addressed. Empathy is not an attempt to explore what the person might be only half-saying or saying implicitly. The skill of empathy involves translating your understanding of the person's experiences, behaviours and feelings into a response that communicates this.

Three steps are involved in empathy: listening, understanding and communicating to the other person that you understand. In order to respond empathically, you must ask yourself, 'What is the main message being expressed in terms of feelings, and the experiences and behaviours that underlie these feelings?' Once you think that you have identified the main message, check out your understanding with the other person.

'You feel .... because ....' is the simplest form of expressing empathy to another person.

'You feel ....' is to be followed by a statement of the emotion expressed by the person.

For example,

'You feel hurt...'

'You feel angry...'

'You feel annoyed...'

You are attempting to identify the emotion and the degree of intensity. A person may express anger at being treated unfairly by a manager. The feeling component you are interested in is the feeling of anger that is being expressed.

The 'because' is followed by an indication of the experiences and/or behaviours that underlie the person's feelings.

For example,

'You feel sad because moving means leaving all your friends.'

'You feel anxious because you don't know what's happening.'

'You feel relieved because you passed your assignment.'

The person will automatically reply, confirming, or denying and correcting, the empathic statement made by the mediator and continue the communication. When the mediator again responds with an empathic statement, the communication continues. The exact words are not important, as they merely provide a framework for communicating understanding to the other person. This framework is particularly useful as a training exercise.

However, you will most likely find when you are practising as a mediator that you will use whatever wording seems most appropriate to the person you are communicating with. If you are empathic in the way you present yourself to the people you work with, they will not be put off by occasional inaccuracies on your part. When empathy is used, the problem situation becomes increasingly clearer in terms of specific experiences, behaviours and feelings. It is important to note that, unlike specific questions, it is the participant who is leading the conversation, not the mediator.

There are a number of ways to improve the quality of empathic responses. These include allowing yourself time to think, keeping responses short and tailoring them to the person. Before responding, it is important to listen and reflect on what the person has said. This does not necessarily mean losing your spontaneity. Do not make speeches or encourage the other person to ramble. You want to engage the person in meaningful dialogue. This is best done by using frequent short responses. This is particularly important in situations where English might not be a first language, and is crucial when using interpreters. Tailoring your response to the other person requires cultural sensitivity and awareness, and being responsive to the person's emotional tone, posture and language. Match your responses without mimicking or being disrespectful of the other person. Some common problems to avoid in communicating empathy are not responding, asking a question, using clichés, providing an interpretation, pretending to understand, or parroting a response. Moving to action is also not helpful because the focus should remain on listening and understanding. Empathy is used well when it assists people to explore their experiences, behaviours and feelings and to gain a better understanding of the relationships between each of these.

The quality of empathic responses can be evaluated according to how they have helped develop and maintain a good working relationship with the person. Empathic responses are also considered effective if they help the person explore the problem situation in terms of relevant feelings, experiences and behaviours more fully. If a person is easily threatened or is made uncomfortable by a discussion of her or his feelings, you may want to emphasise experiences and behaviours, and proceed only gradually to a discussion of feelings. You might also suggest to the participant how you might feel yourself if placed in a similar situation. Males are often not used to discussing their feelings, particularly with a stranger.[7] For some people, fear of intimacy is part of the problem. This can include the kind of intimacy that might be involved in the relationship with the worker. Since empathy is a kind of intimacy, too much empathy too soon can inhibit rather than facilitate communication. Warmth, closeness and intimacy are not the main goals. The goal of the relationship is to help people explore themselves and the conflict. If empathy stands in the way of this goal, it should be avoided.

In pairs, one person is to make the following statement as if they really mean it and the other person is to respond with an empathic response. Take turns.

1. *I really worry about how I'll manage financially if I leave him. The kids are still young and I haven't worked for the past six years.*

Empathic response (feeling and content):

2. *I didn't mean to hurt anyone. I really didn't. You have to believe me. I just needed the money.*

Empathic response (feeling and content):

To practise and reinforce this skill, the empathy ball game can also be used as a warm up activity at the start of a class. The empathy ball game provides spontaneity, and requires full concentration as you do not know who the ball will be thrown to next.

Once you have mastered empathic responses combine these with skills in reframing, discussed later in this chapter under Mediation stage 4: identification of main issues: agenda setting, to provide what is referred as an advanced accurate empathy response. Reframing explores other possibilities and questions intentions.

Empathy ball game

Sit in a circle. One person makes a statement about how they feel today and reasons why and then throws the ball to another person in the circle. He or she responds with an empathic response. Wait for the person to confirm or deny that the response was accurate. They then make a statement about how they are feeling today and reasons why and throw the ball to another person. This process continues until everyone has had a turn.

Mediation stage 3: storytelling

In the storytelling stage of the mediation, each party has the opportunity to tell her or his story uninterrupted. It is beneficial for the mediator and other parties to listen to the issues and concerns confronting each party, and the contingency issues that are important to each of them, as these will effect later negotiations. Telling their story and in particular listening provides each party with an opportunity to gain a more in-depth understanding of, and perspective on, the issues facing each party and how their behaviours impact upon each other.

Participants may be concerned that in providing details of their needs and interests to other parties they may be weakening their bargaining position. However, the opposite is the case, as sharing information reduces unanticipated risks and makes it possible later on to reach a negotiated outcome. If all parties provide information that is crucial to the resolution of the conflict, and if the mediator has conducted thorough fact finding, potential benefits for each party in resolving the conflict are maximised.

Do you think that sharing information about needs, interests and concerns weakens or strengthens bargaining positions? Provide examples of both.

Storytelling is an important stage in the mediation process. This may be the first time that the person has had the opportunity to do so uninterrupted, and more importantly it may be the first time that other parties in the dispute have listened to how the person has been affected by the conflict. To achieve this, the setting must be conducive to the parties paying full attention to each other. Mediators manage the process so as not to allow interruptions, making sure that each party has equal time.

Often, people will respond to accusations made by a party who has spoken before them. The mediator will encourage the parties to avoid doing this, but rather to tell their own stories and how they understand what has happened, and how they have been affected.

Language is of crucial importance as it is the main medium used in comunication. This includes all forms of language, both spoken and unspoken. Storytelling, even to a single listener, can have a profound effect on a person's sense of self, which is so reliant upon memories.8 Memories give rise to a number of questions that may or may not be shared openly. These might include, What were my alternatives? Where did I go wrong? How did all this start? Could I have done things differently? It is important to be sensitive to the psychological impact that memories may have and the associated meanings given to the interaction between the parties in dispute and the worker. People remember events that they have experienced personally, but other recollections are 'second-hand' knowledge of things that have happened to other people. It is particularly at these points that the memories of people familiar with the person, event or place being described are sought in an attempt to see the similarities and differences in interpretation. This will give an indication of whether the person's account is generally accepted, or very much her or his own individual view and interpretation of events.

1. *Mediators will often suggest things parties might do instead of interrupting. What might these be?*
2. *You have asked all parties not to interrupt, as well as employing the suggestions you have listed above. However one party continually interrupts and interjects while the other person is talking? What would you do?*
3. *Additional information on interrupting party: the person who is interrupting is an Aboriginal woman elder. The person who is being interrupted by her is a thirty-five-year-old man of Anglo-Australian background. He is a mining company representative. The conflict is about mining operations on a sacred Indigenous site.*
4. *What are the power issues in this dispute?*

5. *Apply critical theory: how might this woman be discriminated against or oppressed?*
6. *How would you respond now, given this new information?*

When listening to people's stories, we are listening for multiple meanings and interpretations. The critical theories discussed in chapter 4 assist in analysing discourses according to power, positions, meanings, behaviours and value differences. Some of these may challenge professional expertise.

Consciousness-raising and discourse analysis

Consciousness-raising links the personal and political to increase awareness of the structures and discourses that contribute to oppression. Awareness creates opportunities for action. Consciousness-raising may inadvertently be oppressive if it is based on the assumption that the mediator's consciousness is superior to that of the parties in the dispute. This needs to be a mutual process, not one that is imposed. The main features of consciousness-raising are shared expertise, respect and active listening.

Practices for changing consciousness include dialogical relationships, with power shared as much as possible between the parties.9 This is underpinned by a belief that each party has equivalent expertise. Professional knowledge does not have more status than the knowledge of the parties. Shared understandings of political and social dimensions to problems are developed. Consciousness-raising and discourse analysis encourage self-reflection and critical questioning. Self-reflexive practice is crucial for the avoidance of domination. This requires awareness of use of self in determining and changing a situation. Mediators are required to reflect upon and question their own practices in terms of claims to knowledge and power and authority. Reflection on use of self includes consideration of how the mediator's cultural and social background, personal history, values and assumption, personality and emotions impact upon the mediation.

Critical questioning is used to look at external factors impacting upon a conflict situation and opens up different ways of viewing a situation. It can assist in deconstructing negative views and stereotypes. Deconstruction looks at different meanings within the relevant context and provides opportunities to explore social expectations and behaviours. In doing so, it allows for reconstruction of new ideas and beliefs.

Questions are a normal part of everyday interaction and inquiry. Questions are generally categorised as open or closed. In a mediation session, closed questions are used to gain factual information, or to bring a conversation to a close. Open questions are used to encourage storytelling and sharing of ideas. If a question can be answered briefly or with a 'yes' or 'no' response, it is a closed question. Funnel questions are those that follow a particular idea in a broad sense and then narrow down to specifics. Critical questioning requires recognition of both internalised oppression and internalised domination and how this impacts upon a person's behaviour generally as well as during conflict situations. Internalised oppression focuses on the incorporation of dominant social ideas and prejudices and how this can result in low self-esteem and feelings of powerlessness and inferiority. Internalised domination is the opposite of internalised oppression and focuses on the dominant group accepting prejudices, and acting on these by feeling and behaving in a superior and powerful manner.[10]

Narratives and strengths perspectives are particularly useful. They assist consciousness-raising and discourse analysis in the storytelling stage of mediation because they value the uniqueness of individual experience, focus on individual meanings and identify dominant discourses and impacts. Narratives are useful for developing stories and conceptualisations that challenge the status quo. Strengths perspectives are empowering as they focus on potential strengths and capacities and not limitations.

Reflect on ways you oppress others and ways in which others oppress you. What personal features and contexts make you feel powerful or powerless?

Probes are particularly useful during storytelling. Probes are statements that encourage people to talk and clarify. Probes do not need to be questions. Too many questions can give a person a feeling of being interrogated. Probes can be verbal questions and statements, or simply restating the last one or two words the person has just said. Probes also include what are referred to as minimal encouragers such as 'uh huh', 'yes', 'I see', 'oh'. Probes can be non-verbal behaviours such as nodding, maintaining appropriate eye contact and leaning forward to display interest. Two general principles when using probes are

1. Once you have used a probe, let the other person take the initiative in exploring their situation. Listening is very important.
2. Use a paraphrase rather than another probe or a series of probes as a way of encouraging further exploration of the situation.

Mediation stage 4: identification of main issues: agenda setting

A common problem for beginning mediators is that they list all of the problems for each party that were expressed during storytelling. When it comes to identifying the main issues, separate lists of issues are presented for each party. What is needed is one list of issues that are common to all of the parties expressed in neutral and non-threatening language. This is often referred to as agenda-setting and is the basis for future negotiations. Rather than developing separate lists for each party, it is important that the issues identified are mutual and shared by all parties. However, if there are issues that are important to one party only, the mediator will include these on the list with the agreement of both parties. It is essential that there is agreement that these are the main issues in contention. The issues are then set out in a mutually accepted order of priority so that they each can be explored separately. This makes complex multi-party disputes more manageable while at the same time recognising the complex interplay between each of the main issues. Beginning with a mutual issue, rather than an individual one, is preferred, to encourage mutuality and joint problem-solving, and to avoid perceptions of bias.

Reframing

In conflict resolution, reframing is a useful skill for identifying main issues and developing new perspectives that lead to the development of a common vision and new ways of communicating. Reframing is neutralising a negative statement or issue. It is neither agreeing nor disagreeing but rather seeing it differently. Reframing assists in shifting people's views and perspectives of a problem situation by allowing for different interpretations and possibilities. If this shift in thinking and perception does not occur, it is unlikely that an agreement will successfully be negotiated and implemented. Reframing removes the intensity of emotion from a statement as well as allocation of blame. Reframing responses are stated in neutral non-blaming and non-judgemental language. They are spoken in a questioning tone of voice and suggest other possible interpretations. The focus is on the issue not the person.

A complaint was lodged to the CEO of a community health centre by the coordinator of an older persons' activity group called the Friendship Group. They complained that members of the youth activity group were moving the furniture in the room where they held their weekly meetings. They did not like them storing their pool tables and table tennis tables against the walls in the room as they feared they would fall down and injure one of their members. Members of the Friendship Group were also very unhappy with the noise level of the groups when they were using the medical services provided at the centre. They worried that they might be bowled over by a young person running around the centre.

The coordinator of the youth activity group argued that the young people were entitled to use the centre, and that the equipment in the room was set up and stored away each night after use. She argued that the centre was essentially a community centre and that the young people should be allowed to have fun even if this generally meant making noise as well. She did not feel that the noise was excessive for a group of this nature. She felt the Friendship Group was trying to keep the room for their own exclusive use, or for quiet activities and that this was not reasonable.

The CEO asked a social worker at the centre to mediate between the coordinators of both groups. The main issues identified were

- use of shared space
- safety.

The mediator felt that use of shared space included the shared activity room and the different activities such as the activity group and the medical services. This also picked up on the issue of noise levels in the centre.

Safety covered concerns raised about the equipment falling over as well as the fear of older people being knocked over by young people running around the centre. Both parties agreed that use of shared space and safety were the main issues.

Reframing can be used throughout the mediation process and is not limited to identifying main issues.

Examples of reframing are as follows.

Statement: The neighbours don't care if their barking dog keeps us awake all night.

Reframe: The barking dog is keeping you awake at night.

'Dog' may simply be listed as a main issue.

Statement: All the builder cares about is getting our money and when his next holiday is. He doesn't care about quality workmanship.

Reframe: The quality of the house is not what you expected.

'Quality of house' might be listed as a main issue.

Reframe the following statements:
Statement: She just doesn't seem to care. She never answers her email or returns telephone messages. I know important things are not being done but she pretends that they are.
Reframe:

Statement: They just rang the council and arranged to have the tree on our nature strip cut down without even talking to us about it.

Reframe:

Removing the emotional content can remove the sting and neutralise the problem and make it easier to deal with. In private session, reframing is often used in conjunction with empathy. Empathy responds to the emotional content, with reframing questioning intentions and exploring other possibilities. This is sometimes referred to as advanced accurate empathy.[11]

Particularly in situations of ongoing relationships, it is often important that developing new perspectives is not seen as giving in, or an admission of guilt or error, but rather the opening up other possible ways of viewing and managing conflict. This serves to maintain the dignity of each party and to save face. In other situations, an apology or admission of guilt is necessary before parties feel able to move on. An admission of guilt is a key feature of conflict resolution processes in the criminal justice area, particularly reintegrative shaming, discussed in chapter 7. This is an important consideration, particularly as it can stop an agreement from being reached if it is not resolved.

Do you think there are situations where it is important for parties to admit error or guilt? If yes, what are they? If no, why not?

Conclusion

The problem-defining phase includes the mediation stages of intake, orientation, storytelling and identification of main issues. Intake includes assessing whether or not mediation is appropriate and identifying the conflict management goal of each party. If it is deemed appropriate the mediator decides who should participate, and in what capacity. The mediation commences with orientation by the mediator to the process, and rules of engagement by the parties. It is important that the parties express a commitment to the process and rules, or that modifications are made that are acceptable to all parties, including the mediator. This may simply be an adjustment of the length of the session or inclusion of more breaks. Separate sessions are conducted to screen for possible violence and issues not revealed that may prevent effective negotiations later on. Empathy is a particularly useful skill during private session as it communicates understanding of the person's feelings, behaviours and experiences. Each party has the opportunity to tell her or his story un-interrupted in the storytelling stage of the mediation. Consciousness-raising and discourse analysis are useful for identifying power imbalances and possible areas of oppression, as well as for developing respectful relationships, effective listening and the sharing of expertise. Reframing is a useful skill for identifying main issues, particularly those shared by all parties in neutral, non-blaming language, as well as being applicable to other stages of the mediation process.

In the next chapter, the second phase of the mediation process, problem-solving, is presented.

6

Problem Solving

After completion of the problem defining phase of mediation, with the main issues identified and agreed to by all parties, the mediation process moves into the second phase – problem solving. The different stages in phase 2 are discussed in this chapter, commencing with stage 5: developing options: mapping the conflict. This is followed by selecting options through negotiation and decision-making. An agreement is then reached and an implementation strategy devised, including review and evaluation mechanisms.

Mediation stage 5: developing options: mapping the conflict

It is useful to map the conflict by identifying key players and their interests, needs, concerns and fears. This is particularly useful in gaining a clearer understanding of the conflict when faced with entrenched and apparently intractable conflict. Mapping the conflict involves awareness and careful listening to understand the conflict in terms of its constituent, attitudinal, behavioural and situational components.

It is sometimes difficult to identify who is actually involved in the conflict. You may recall the example of the dispute at the neighbourhood house in chapter 1. The four people referred all denied involvement in the conflict and claimed that there must have been a mistake. This is not uncommon. This denial may be quite correct in that he or she may be the wrong person. It can also be a powerful defence mechanism: overtly denying the problem exists can be a good way of avoiding having to deal with it. For the party who has the most power, this may be preferable, as they can continue on without any interference. Or denial may be used by a less powerful party due to a lack of trust in the mediator or mediation process, and fear of possible repercussions.

Amberley first met Royce at work in an information technology sales company. Royce was a sales and marketing manager and Amberley worked in direct sales. Royce was Amberley's line manager. They started going out together and eventually Amberley moved in with Royce's family. This was not planned; Amberley arrived in tears on the doorstep of Royce's family's home one night, saying she had had a fight with the woman she shared a house with and could not return home. Amberley needed somewhere to stay. Royce's mother took pity on her and told her she could stay as long as she liked.

One year later, Amberley was still living with Royce and his family. She was very keen to settle down and have a family and announced to members of Royce's family she was going overseas to have a wedding dress made. The family thought this was an announcement of their engagement but wondered about the casual manner in which they had been told. When they congratulated Royce on the good news, he denied any knowledge of it.

Amberley began to complain about Royce taking advantage of her and not making plans to settle down. She complained that he was spending less and less time with her.

Amberley had sold her car; she felt she no longer needed it as Royce had one. They drove to and from work together. However, Royce often worked longer hours than Amberley and was required to attend meetings late in the day and of an evening. Amberley resented having to wait around for Royce to finish at the end of the day or having to make her own way home.

Eventually, Royce decided to break off the relationship with Amberley. However, she remained living in his house and they also continued to work together. She became very angry with Royce and started speaking rudely to him at work or ignoring him completely. This interfered with relations amongst the work group and ultimately productivity; the general manager told Royce and Amberley not to bring their private problems to work. The problems continued, so the general manager suggested that Amberley consider moving to an interstate branch of the company. Amberley was outraged at this suggestion and refused. The general manager did not really want to lose her or Royce, as both were high-performing employees. He decided to refer the matter to mediation.

When Amberley was contacted by the mediator, she denied any problems, claiming that she and Royce had sorted out their differences; they had been going out together in the past, but they were now good friends. Amberley felt they had a very good working relationship and mediation was not necessary. The general manager told her she had no choice and that he required her to attend if she wanted to remain with the company. Royce was agreeable to attending mediation.

1. *What are the power issues in this dispute?*
2. *Why do you think Amberley did not want to participate in a mediation session with Royce?*
3. *Do you think it is appropriate to agree to mediate this dispute?*
4. *The general manager offers the company boardroom as the venue for the mediation. Do you accept this offer?*

Mapping the conflict is useful particularly when it is hard to identify the actual parties or issues in dispute. This may be because the conflict is very complex, with multiple parties involved. It may also be due to limited resources in resolving the conflict.

Three steps involved in mapping the conflict are

Step 1: defining the issue
Step 2: identify who is involved
Step 3: list the major needs, concerns and fears of each party.[1]

The main issues between Royce and Amberley were identified in the following order:

- working relations
- personal relationship
- income security
- housing.

The conflict between Royce and Amberley is mapped below for the issue of working relations. The parties agreed that, as it was workplace mediation, working relations took priority. The mediator was also mindful that other issues might be resolved by attending to the work relationship first.

Figure 6.1

Conflict Map

Who: Amberley
Needs: Secure employment
Concerns: Job security, financial, reputation
Fears: She will lose her job.

Who: Manager		**Who:** Royce
Needs: Productivity		**Needs:** Respect, authority.
Concerns: Tension in the workplace will reduce productivity.	**Issue:** Working relations	**Concerns:** Feels belittled, undermined and embarrassed in front of other staff.
Fears: Loss of productivity; does not want to lose Royce as management has invested a lot of time and money in him.		**Fears:** Amberley wil continue to undermine him and his position in the organisation.

Mapping the conflict highlights who may have the most to gain and who may in fact be more vulnerable in the mediation process. This is particularly highlighted when looking at fears. In this scenario, Amberley seems to have the most to lose. Although the manager does not want to lose either of them, he is prepared to let her go, but not Royce. Amberley's fear is losing her job; Royce fears ongoing harassment by Amberley.

Once the conflict has been mapped, the main issues identified and the needs, concerns and fears of each party listed, the next step is to ensure that each party has the necessary information to generate and develop viable options.

Options are created by using a variety of techniques. These include

- breaking down the problem into smaller more manageable components
- identifying the desired outcome
- trial and error
- maintaining the status quo but generating greater commitment and enforcement
- going with the obvious solution
- brainstorming.[2]

Different methods are appropriate for different circumstances. For example, going with the obvious solution or a trial and error approach may be more appropriate for a less complex issue, or one involving few people, or limited resources, risks or consequences.

Dividing up the problem, brainstorming or identifying the desired outcome may be more suited to a complex issue, or one involving many people, resources, risks and consequences. The key to the success of generated options is the level of commitment by all parties, how well participants' needs are met, and to what extent they have been included in designing that option. Designing options is a process that requires different tools at different times. For instance, halfway through brainstorming, it may become evident that another approach is more appropriate.

Designing options is not a linear process. A number of different approaches may be tried in any order. It is not necessarily complex, because sometimes people easily agree to an obvious solution. Good analysis is essential for developing effective solutions. The strategy of 'go slow to go fast' often sits uneasily with pressure for instant solutions. Intervention based on faulty or wrong analysis is likely to exacerbate rather than alleviate both the presenting and the underlying problems. Analysing each option according to strengths, weaknesses, opportunities and threats, also known as SWOT analysis, is useful in testing its viability.

In the case of Royce and Amberley, focusing on the issue of workplace relations alone has already partialised the problem. Other issues such as housing are not dealt with yet. While related, they are dealt with separately. This separation allows for in-depth focus on one issue at a time, making each one more manageable. Identifying each desired outcome provides a goal for the later negotiations and keeps the mediation on track.

The mediator here explored different relationships with Royce and Amberley using Ricci's (1997) classification of relationships according to the purpose of the relationship and levels of associated intimacy. These relationships are

- acquaintance or business
- friendship
- positive intimacy
- negative intimacy.

Acquaintance or business relationships are characterised by formal courtesies with low levels of personal disclosure. Agreements are explicit, with public, structured meetings and high levels of personal privacy.

Friendships are characterised by trust, respect, understanding, increased assumptions and expectations. Increased levels of emotional attachment and personal disclosure occur, as more private time is spent together.

Positive intimacy involves affirming assumptions and expectations and implicit agreements. The relationship is an informal one and is characterised by support and cooperation, with intense feelings and emotions. There are high levels of self-disclosure trust, respect and loyalty.

Negative intimacy is the exact opposite of positive intimacy. Although the relationship is still informal and agreements are implicit, the expectations and assumptions are now negative. Distrust, disloyalty and disrespect feature; confidences are betrayed, often in order to inflict hurt on the other person. Feelings are intensely competitive rather than cooperative.[3]

It is important to consider the type of relationship parties want, or need to have in the future. For couples like Amberley and Royce who have moved from positive intimacy to negative intimacy, the goal is not to restore positive intimacy but rather to establish a business relationship.

Brainstorming was used to generate as many solutions as possible. The mediator asked Royce and Amberley to think of any solutions that immediately came to mind. The mediator wrote these on the outside of the conflict map as they were said, without any discussion of their feasibility. Spontaneity, creativity and energy were generated because the approach of 'anything goes' within reason was adopted. The options thought of by Amberley and Royce were

1. one of them leave the company
2. Amberley accept the transfer offered to her
3. both of them leave the company
4. one of them transfer to a different branch of the company
5. both of them transfer to different branches
6. both of them stay with the company in the same location
7. an internal management restructure so that Amberley is not working directly to Royce
8. Amberley and Royce agree to communicate only about business matters in a respectful and businesslike manner when in the workplace.

Before moving into this next stage of the process, it is often useful to conduct a private session to check with parties whether anything might prevent them from selecting options and negotiating an agreement. The mediator asked both Royce and Amberley in private if there was anything that they were aware of that might prevent them from reaching a negotiated outcome. Both answered in the negative. The private session also provided an opportunity for the mediator to check out levels of comfort with the mediation so far and to provide coaching in the communication skills required for effective negotiations, particularly assertive behaviours. The mediator felt that both Amberley and Royce needed coaching in assertive behaviours if they were to negotiate effectively with each other.

Mediation stage 6: selecting options: negotiation

The parties are now selecting options. They are communicating directly with each other, with assistance from the mediator as required. This stage is also known as assisted negotiation. The seating configuration has been changed; parties now face each other and communicate directly. The process also becomes less formal as the parties work through the different options and decide on which are most suitable.

Selecting options involves bringing order to the range of options generated in the designing options stage, and making links between similar or complementary options. Selecting options also has an evaluative component, in that the appropriateness and feasibility of particular options are assessed. The focus of selecting options is to match options to needs,identified during the mapping process. Preferred options are those that meet most or many of the needs of all parties, and take account of many of their fears and concerns.

The principle of least contest assumes shared, rather than competing interests. It is based on the premise of 'use the least force necessary'. Negotiations commence with private discussions and only escalate to other more adversarial methods if conciliatory approaches do not succeed. Interventions from the least to greatest contest are

- private talk
- group representation
- campaigns
- protests
- negative publicity.

It is important to be mindful of the negative consequences of more threatening types of action. It is the mediator's role to assist people to make informed decisions and consider best and worst possible outcomes. The mediator must respect client decisions and client self-determination. However, the mediator is responsible for ensuring that decisions and agreements reached in mediation are fair and equitable for all parties. In the mediation with Royce and Amberley private talks were sufficient for reaching a suitable outcome.

The process for selecting options involves four steps.

Step 1:   Link the options that go together in some way.

Step 2:   Evaluate the options generated according to the 'best alternative to a negotiated agreement' (BATNA) and 'worst alternative to a negotiated agreement' (WATNA) of each party.

Step 3:   Eliminate the inappropriate ones.

Step 4:   Put the rest in the order in which they need to be implemented.[4]

It is important to try to choose options that meet most needs. This process results in a range of solutions to a particular problem rather than one answer. In step 1 with Royce and Amberley, options, 6, 7, and 8 were linked because they focused on both Amberley and Royce remaining with the company at the same location.

In step 2 the first three stages of the mutual gains approach discussed earlier in chapter 3 was useful for selecting and evaluating the viability of different options. The four stages in this approach are

1. preparation
2. value creation
3. value distribution
4. follow-through.

In the preparation stage, each party considers the 'best alternative to a negotiated agreement' (BATNA) and the 'worst alternative to a negotiated agreement' (WATNA). It is also useful for parties to consider the BATNA and WATNA of other parties. As neither Royce nor Amberley felt they had a better alternative to a negotiated agreement, there was now a stronger commitment to the mediation process. Both clearly identified a worst alternative if they did not settle their differences. For Amberley, her WATNA was losing her job and for Royce it was continually being undermined and the possibility of lost opportunity for promotion.

Value creation involves exploring the interests of parties to see if there are differences in what they attach value to and, where variations occur, how these might be traded. Both Amberley and Royce attached similar value to the same things, so trading did not occur. They valued the possibility of the creation of a new management structure that meant they no longer worked directly with each other.

Value distribution focuses on fair outcomes for all parties so that all benefit equally. It is important that the options selected do not favour one party more so than another.

In step 3 of selecting options, options 1 to 5 were eliminated, as both Amberley and Royce clearly wanted to stay with the company and not change locations. Step 4 involved ordering the options for implementation. It was decided that according to option 6 both of them remain with the company in the same location. While both agreed that option 7 – an internal management restructure so that Amberley would not be working directly to Royce – was desirable, it might not be possible. They would pursue this with the general manager, but they agreed that option 8, according to which Amberley and Royce would communicate in a respectful and businesslike manner when in the workplace could be implemented immediately. This resulted in a reordering of the options.

1. Both of them stay with the company in the same location.
2. Amberley and Royce agree to communicate only about business matters in a respectful and businesslike manner when in the workplace.
3. An internal management restructure would be carried out so that Amberley would not be working directly to Royce.

These three options met all of the needs, concerns and fears of Amberley and Royce, as well as the general manager. Amberley maintained secure employment and financial security, with her reputation not harmed. Royce's fears of Amberley continuing to undermine him were allayed by a commitment to respectful communication in the workplace from Amberley. This responded to his need for respect and authority in the workplace from Amberley and the other staff. The general manager was pleased with the agreed options as he felt they would result in more positive communication and less tension in the workplace, thereby contributing to increased productivity. He was very pleased to keep two valued members of staff. It wasn't necessary to repeat the process for the other issues identified, as these had been inadvertently addressed by focusing on the working relations issue. The personal relationship was covered by looking at the most appropriate type of working relationship between Royce and Amberley. Income security was answered. Amberley announced that she was in the process of arranging other accommodation and planned to move out of Royce's family home shortly.

Mediation stage 7: agreement

Discovering a common vision or goals and compatible interests is central to the conflict resolution process. New procedures are often required where previous ones have not been useful or adequate in resolving the conflict. Changes in future relationships are necessary for improved communications to occur; people need to be mindful of both rights and responsibilities. Clarification of the interplay between rights and entitlements is important as in conflict situations people become preoccupied with their own rights and forget about the rights of others or the responsibilities that come with rights.

An understanding of respective sources of power and leverage in relationships can assist in developing ways of managing these and working cooperatively (see chapter 2).

Finding a common enemy is less obvious and seems in a way to be unfair or punitive or even a shirking of responsibility. It can, however, create a sense of cohesion and purpose that might not otherwise exist.

It is important that this solution be implemented according to the principle of 'no harm' and that innocent parties are not made scapegoats in the process. It is preferable if the common enemy is of an abstract nature such as 'the system' rather than an individual. Finding a common enemy can assist parties to save face and move on.[5]

Apart from finding a common enemy, all these factors were present in the mediation between Royce and Amberley. Amberley correctly perceived she was in a weaker position than Royce. This was influenced by a number of factors, including gender, age, position in the organisation and length of employment. Royce was in a more senior position and had greater power than Amberley, but he clearly felt his position was threatened. Royce ultimately did have more leverage than Amberley due his greater level of power and ultimately knowing that, if it was a choice between him and Amberley, he would remain.

Different practices occur with the recording of agreements. Some mediators prefer to prepare a written agreement to be signed by the mediator and the parties. This generally includes an implementation plan with feedback, review and monitoring mechanisms. However, other mediators prefer to leave it to the parties to keep their own records of decisions made and to follow up with their solicitors if they want to make decisions made at a mediation legally binding.

A written agreement was prepared by the mediator for Amberley and Royce to sign. This included the decisions made at mediation and how they were to be implemented. The general manager agreed to change Amberley's supervision arrangements. This was easily done, and did not require any major restructure. It was decided that these changes would take effect immediately; a further session with the mediator was arranged in a fortnight's time to review the implementation of the agreement.

Mediation stage 8: implementation and follow-up

The ultimate success of a mediation or conflict resolution process is in its outcomes. This will be determined by how appropriate they are, as well as how they are implemented. If the agreement reached at mediation is not implemented, the problems are likely to continue and people will feel disheartened or betrayed by the process, and will be less likely to commit in the future.

Strategies aimed at the enforcement of agreements, whether verbal or written, are necessary. It is important that an action plan is developed that includes the recognition of joint and individual responsibilities, and that tasks are assigned to particular people. The possible restructuring of existing organisations or the establishment of new organisations and structures may be required, accompanied by appropriate resource allocation. A time frame for implementation is necessary with feedback, review and monitoring mechanisms. If this is achieved, there will be greater confidence in the process and people will be more likely to commit in the future.

At the review meeting, it turned out that the different manager for Amberley had been problematic, as this person did not have the required knowledge and experience. Both Amberley and Royce felt they could work effectively if the management role was transferred back to Royce and that in terms of productivity this was the preferred arrangement. The general manager was agreeable to changing the management structure once more, and a further review session was arranged two weeks later. At that meeting, it was reported that things were working well. Amberley mentioned she had moved into her own accommodation.

A year later, they are still working amicably together. However, Royce swears he will never again go out with someone he manages.

Conclusion

The focus of phase 2 of the mediation process is on problem-solving. This includes developing options and mapping the conflict followed by selecting options through negotiation and decision making. An agreement is prepared, with an implementation strategy that includes review and evaluation mechanisms. Mapping the conflict to identify the main issues and needs, concerns and fears of each party helps to gain a clearer understanding of the conflict. The next step is to ensure that each party has the necessary information to generate and develop viable options and to decide on a process of how this will be done. Once the options have been developed, preferred options are chosen. This selection is based on options that meet most or many of the needs of all parties and takes account of many or most of their fears and concerns. An agreement is reached that generally includes an implementation plan with feedback, review and monitoring mechanisms.

The next chapter looks at main areas of mediation practice.

7

Fields of Practice

In conflict management and mediation, a number of groups have practised formally and informally over many centuries – for example, in ancient China, where community leaders were responsible for resolving
disputes.[1] This practice also occurs in many Indigenous communities.[2]
The development of neighbourhood mediation has its origins in grass
roots participation. Early mediators had no formal training or education
in mediation or conflict management. What they did share, however,
was the respect and power vested in them by their community. Mediation is practised, in various degrees of intensity and structure, informally
in most professions that deal with people. Since the late twentieth century, an industry has developed around conflict management, with increasing training requirements for mediators. The main professional
groups practising as mediators are lawyers, social workers and psychologists and planners.[3] Other mediators include chaplains, drug and alcohol counsellors, youth workers, police officers, recreation officers,
school teachers, occupational health rehabilitation counsellors, accoun-
tants, engineers, architects, and real estate agents.[4]

Areas of practice include parent–adolescent, family and adult–elder
mediation. In Australia, planners are required to undergo training in
mediation and conflict management; mediation is practised in planning, environment, building and construction, property and neighbourhood disputes. Mediation is increasingly being used in
organisations and workplaces, including recreational and sporting
leagues and education and training settings, with schools introducing

models of peer mediation. Criminal matters as well as personal injury disputes are also being referred to mediation.[5]

Mediators often practise in a wide range of areas; for instance, an estate agent was advertising services in property mediation as well as parent–adolescent mediation.[6] Due to the diverse backgrounds of mediators and their variety of perspectives, it has proved difficult to develop agreement on definitions, goals and methods of mediation. Regulation has come from the requirements embedded in legislation, employers' terms and conditions and prerequisites for registration with different mediation associations. Professional associations also have mandatory requirements or suggested guidelines for practice.[7]

In this chapter, main areas and models of mediation practice are discussed, including, family, parent–adolescent, adult–elder, workplace, criminal justice, neighbourhood and planning disputes. The following chapter is devoted to complex multiparty environmental disputes.

Family mediation

There has been an increasing use of family dispute resolution over the past three decades in Australia, Britain, the United States and Canada. This has been supported in legislative changes. In Australia, it is mandatory to attend a family dispute resolution meeting before the commencement of court proceedings. Mandatory mediation is not enforced in situations of known child abuse and other forms of violence, or if it is not possible for all parties to participate effectively in the family dispute resolution process. However, in cases where this is not known, situations of violence may be dealt with at mediation. The lower costs associated with family dispute resolution may mean that some women in abusive relationships may choose this as it is a cheaper alternative to litigation.[8]

A dispute resolution worker may, however, assess that family dispute resolution is not appropriate due to imbalances in bargaining power.[9] Concerns have been expressed about the appropriateness of screening techniques and the suitability of mediation in situations where violence is an issue.[10] Therapeutic mediation is often used in family disputes due to the focus on ongoing parenting relationships.[11] As pointed out in chapter 3, the main objective of therapeutic mediation is to improve relationships between parties by dealing with underlying causes of conflict. The dispute is defined in terms of relationships, emotions and behaviours. Time and cost pressures, however, mean that evaluative models, and not therapeutic models, dominate in family mediation. Evaluative models focus on legal rights and entitlements with precedents used to inform parties of how courts have decided similar matters in the past.

Marriage is a social, legal and, for many, religious institution that underpins various government policies. It is a public declaration of a person's love and commitment to another person and to their relationship and is something that is generally not taken lightly. At some point in their lives, most people fill the criteria of being single, married or divorced; the never-married are still in the great minority. Adults today are more cautious due to experiences in their own families and those of their friends. They can see that, for some, marriage has clearly not worked and they do not want to make the same mistakes as their parents. People are still forming relationships and cohabitating; however, it is the next step (marriage) that they are cautions about. The declining marriage rates of young people must be seen within the context of broader social and economic changes affecting these young people's lives. For males especially, there are tremendous expectations once they are married. These are to provide financially and to buy a house. For many, as young adults, this is not readily achievable and is aggravated by lack of job security today with increased casual and contract appointments and a lack of the long-term employment security their parents enjoyed. For financial reasons, many young people are staying in the family home for extended periods.

Marriage and child-rearing have the potential to provide lifelong companionship and support, meaningful purpose and activity, with increased disposable income generated from dual incomes and shared expenses. Marriage can also create loneliness and poverty, especially for many women who become reliant upon a male's wages. They may feel trapped in an unfulfilling and sometimes abusive relationship from which they see no escape. Many people's needs are not sufficiently met, resulting in high levels of separation and divorce.

Marriage is not suitable for everyone, and those who can have their basic needs met outside of the institution of marriage do well. However, it is generally recognised that women are worse off financially than males in single-parent households.

The focus needs to shift from marriage to other successful relationships in which partners are committed to each other and their offspring. This naturally includes same-sex relationships as well as heterosexual ones. A number of issues that cause conflict in families are financial, gender expectations in terms of roles and responsibilities, different values and beliefs, and lack of trust and respect. The development of future relationships is a focus of family mediation with therapeutic, narrative, transformative and collaborative family law models particularly relevant.[12]

The main features of the collaborative family law model are

- a collaborative contract
- four-way meetings between disputing parties and legal representatives
- a mutual gains approach to negotiations, and
- an enforceable agreement between the parties.[13]

In a collaborative family law process, the parties in dispute, with assistance from their lawyers, draw up a written contract setting down the process and ground rules to be followed and how these will be managed by the parties. Thus the parties are responsible for developing and managing the dispute resolution process. Key elements of the collaborative contract are that the conflict resolution process will be conducted in a fair and equitable manner, with parties given an opportunity to tell their stories uninterrupted. The children's needs are a priority. This is not unlike the opening stages of the mediation process described in chapter 5. However, the key difference is that the parties and their lawyers, rather than an independent neutral third party, are managing the process. A further key difference and central feature of collaborative family law is that the contract includes a statement that the lawyers involved in a collaborative family law process are retained for the sole purpose of assisting in the negotiation of a mutually acceptable agreement. The lawyers are disqualified from representing the parties further if either party decides to go to court. This contract is signed by all parties (lawyers included) before negotiations begin.

Lawyers involve themselves in four-way meetings with the disputing parties in an endeavour to gain a full understanding of the dispute from various perspectives, not just that of their own client. delete Legal advice and information is given about possible outcomes of litigation as well as likely costs involved, with lawyers advocating for the best interests of their clients.

The collaborative family law model incorporates a mutual gains approach to negotiation[14] as well as allowing for full participation by lawyers in both an advisory role on possible outcomes of the dispute and assisting parties in negotiations as 'negotiation coaches'. This includes full disclosure by each party of needs interests and concerns. The best alternative to a negotiated agreement (BATNA) and the worst alternative to a negotiated agreement (WATNA) for each party are considered.

Graham and Annabel had been married for nineteen years and had two children: Sarah, eighteen years old, and Tahlia, fourteen. Both Graham and Annabel worked full time. Tahlia attended a private school and Sarah was now at university. They lived a comfortable middle-class lifestyle. But in recent years the family had grown apart. Annabel was constantly annoyed by Graham leaving things around the house, and not cleaning up after himself. They constantly argued over money even though they were financially comfortable, Graham worried about the short-term contract nature of his work and felt that Annabel had over committed them financially by investing in property and shares. Annabel wanted to renovate the house and buy a new car. Graham, however, refused to spend any money on the house or a new car, saying they couldn't afford it. He accused Annabel of being reckless with their money. Other things about Graham that annoyed Annabel included his drinking and staying out late with his friends that he seemed to find money for, his not helping with the children or the housework, and his snoring that kept her awake at night.

Annabel became increasingly annoyed and angry with Graham and decided she wanted him to leave. She told Graham to go and suggested he live with his mother. She also suggested how they might go about organising their finances. Annabel assumed she would stay in the family home with the children. Graham refused, saying it was his home and if Annabel wanted to leave and go to live with her mother, she was welcome to do so. He would stay and look after the children. Annabel became more and more frustrated with Graham's refusal to leave and sought legal assistance to file for divorce. She and Graham were referred to a family relationship centre for family dispute resolution.

1. *As mediator, what would be the goal of the mediation between Graham and Annabel? Would it be to assist them to separate amicably or to try and resolve their differences and stay together?*

2. *What might be the advantages and disadvantages of having lawyers represent each party and assist in the negotiations?*

Parent–adolescent mediation

In parent–adolescent mediation, peer co-mediation often involves a young person and an adult as mediators. The young person will co-mediate in an endeavour to engage the adolescent in the mediation process.[15] Adolescence is a major developmental stage, in which the adolescent is developing greater independence and individuality. (See chapter 4 on developmental theory.) It is not unusual for parent–adolescent conflict to occur when the young person becomes increasingly assertive and independent, questioning and testing parents' rules and values.[16] Models particularly suited to parent–adolescent conflict are therapeutic, narrative and transformative mediation. A four-session plan, adapted from the mediation model presented in chapter 3, includes

1. The first session is conducted with all family members present.
2. The second session is conducted with the parents or primary caregivers.
3. The third session is conducted with the adolescent.
4. The fourth session is conducted with all family members present.

Session 1 with the family includes introductions, reasons for being at mediation and all family members sharing their stories and perceptions of issues the family is dealing with. Patterns of problem-solving are explored as well as family lifestyle and family culture. Session 2 is private, and is conducted with both parents together and then separately if necessary. This includes information on the adolescent's complete personal history, the parents' relationship history and the personal and family history of each parent. Session 3 is a private session with the adolescent to gain an understanding of awareness of conflict, mood and affect, coping mechanisms and hopes for the future. In session 4, a family interview is conducted once more: here the mediator identifies main issues, maps the conflict and develops options with the family. Negotiations are conducted, preferred options are selected and an agreement is prepared with a plan for implementation and follow-up.

Mandy was thirty-eight years of age and had a twelve-year-old daughter Emily. Emily's father had not had any contact with her since her birth. Mandy and Emily lived in a two-bedroom house. Mandy had not been in another relationship since Emily was born. However, recently she met Jack and fell head over heels in love. Of a weekend, Jack stayed at Mandy's house or she and Emily stayed at Jack's. Jack was divorced and lived alone. He was a professional golfer and had won several tournaments.

Since she had been going out with Jack, Mandy noticed that Emily was becoming increasingly hostile towards him. Things had come to a head recently when they had stayed at Jack's and Emily had snapped the ends off all the golf clubs on Jack's trophies. Mandy was furious with Emily and feared that this might be the end of her relationship with Jack. Mandy sought assistance from mediation, to get Emily to accept her relationship with Jack and to treat him with respect. She wanted Emily to apologise to Jack for what had happened. Emily refused and said she hoped she never saw him again.

As mediator, who do you include in the mediation session? Is it wise to include Jack or is it best to only see Mandy and Emily? What about Emily's father?

How would you decide who to include?

Adult–elder mediation

There is an increased demand for mediation and conflict management with older people and their families, particularly adult children. The goal of adult–elder mediation is to respond to individual, family and social issues while maintaining the dignity and self-determination of the older person.[17] Issues are often in relation to

- living arrangements
- care giving
- financial planning and management
- asset protection
- inheritance/estate disputes
- medical decisions
- family communication
- driving
- guardianship
- administration.

Past relationships between the older person and adult family members are often an indicator of how willing they may or may not be, to be involved in the planning and/or provision of care for an older family member. New strategies are required for working with large, dispersed family groups as well as addressing ethical concerns. Particular challenges of ageing include maintaining independence, coping with loss, care giving and ageing families, and long-term care options for family elders.

People are living longer due to the decline in infant mortality, the control of infectious diseases and improvement in nutrition and living standards. Ageing reflects trends in mortality, frequency of chronic disease and the maintenance of autonomy. Attention to these independent though related variables will increase the proportion of the population surviving disease free to an advanced age. The expected lifespan of individuals is not only likely to increase but the number of years that one is disease-free is also likely to increase. However, the number of years that an older person is expected to live with loss of independence and loss of autonomy is also increasing. Of specific importance to older people are disorders that affect hearing, vision, dental problems, incontinence of urine and faeces, intellectual and cognitive failure and depression. Loneliness is a key factor in compounding health problems, and in particular leading to depression.

The family is seen as the greatest single source of support for older people. However, with increased population mobility, demands of paid employment and responsibility for their own children, adult children are often not spending the time to care, or provide companionship, for their elderly parents. In China, the one-child policy has drastically reduced the number of adult children available to care for elderly parents. On 1 July 2013, the Chinese government amended the Law on Protection of Rights and Interests of the Aged to make it illegal to neglect the 'spiritual needs' of the elderly. It is stipulated that 'children have to visit elderly parents regularly or at least keep in touch with them in some way. Those who don't comply may face prosecution.'[18] Some have argued that the law is not necessary as Chinese people are filial; it is their circumstances that do not allow for more contact. Others argue that forced visits will aggravate relationships that are already strained due to family disputes. Elderly visiting services such as 'chatting, celebrating birthdays and even performances' are available for hire by adult children who are not able to visit in person.[19]

Do you think that legislating for adult children to visit their elderly parents will address the care and companionship needs of older people?

A postmodern view rejects life cycle theory, generational comparisons and positivist views of ageing generally.[20] Rather, postmodernism argues that boundaries between these life stages are fluid. Ageing is viewed as a positive experience, as opposed to modernist views that see it as a time of dependency and physical decline. Postmodernism counters attempts to organise stages of development according to age, refuting images of older age as a time of dependency and decline. A postmodern view is critical of health and welfare workers for their controlling role in access to resources and for fostering a dependency culture among older people.

Mediators are urged to embrace positive images of 'active ageing'. The current context of community care is seen as positive for older people as it gives them more choices and control over what happens to them. Emphasis is placed on difficulties experienced, rather than preconceptions of dependence due to age. From a postmodern perspective, older people have a greater range of positions and identities, including developing new relationships in the areas of work, social, family and sexual relations. The emphasis is on the process of ageing rather than age. A postmodern notion of successful ageing embodies body image, fitness, health and appearance; there is no standard image of old age.

Adult–elder mediation requires consideration of the strengths, capacities and resources of the older person in addition to their needs, concerns, fears and risk factors. The emphasis is on the positive aspects of ageing rather than decline, focusing on maintaining the dignity of the older person providing choices that are consistent with their strengths, potential and desires. Determining the level of risk and developing assessment and flexible packages of care for a select group of older people with health, well-being and social needs is important. Positive choices are highlighted in relation to the type and quality of care required. It is important that the views of the older person and family members are validated in mediation. Forming meaningful partnerships with older people and responding appropriately to their needs, interests, concerns and fears is essential. Mediation requires the establishment of a relationship based on mutual trust and expected reciprocity.

> Mary was in her eighties and had suffered a stroke. She was no longer able to care for herself physically. Her three daughters took it in turns to have Mary at their homes. Mary went to her daughter Elizabeth's at weekends. Elizabeth felt it was too difficult to look after her mother as well as her own family. She had increased her hours of paid work and decided that she could no longer have her mother on weekends. When she told her sisters this, they were extremely angry. Her brother-in-law, the husband of her elder sister, came to her house and insisted that she take her turn in caring for her mother. When Elizabeth refused, he punched her in the face.

Although physical violence is extreme, it exemplifies the tensions that can arise between family members, particularly when high levels of care are involved. It also highlights the family and community expectations that daughters provide care. This makes it difficult for women to refuse to provide care, and to be listened to and respected in having made this decision.[21] It is essential that mediator's develop realistic plans that balance needs and concerns for the older person with respect for the needs and wishes of adult family members. Continuing assessment of care arrangements is required to ascertain suitability and viability.

The relationship developed between the mediator and the older person is paramount. Older people may often be suspicious about outside intervention and reject being perceived as needing help. It is particularly important that time be given to some mutuality of purpose. The mediator needs to work on developing respectful and trusting relationships with both the older person and adult family members. This is sometimes difficult, particularly where there are high levels of conflict among family members. The mediator needs to be clear on whose views are being expressed and how representative these are of other family members. Mediation with families in middle and later life provides major challenges to the skilled mediator. Work with older people and their families interacting with social, health and welfare agencies often involves considerable conflict of both an inter-generational and inter-organisational nature. Strategic intervention is a major adult–elder mediation skill. Advocacy is important when working with older people given the relative under-development and poor quality of many of the services they receive, and the non-existence of appropriate services in some instances. Issues of mediator neutrality need to be considered alongside mediator advocacy.

The older person is seen in the context of a particular social network and environment as a central decision-maker in the health and social situation.[22] Mediation is a collaborative exercise. The older person and their adult family members are aiming at alleviating or ameliorating the older person's presenting and underlying difficulties. The mediator assists the parties to evaluate these difficulties in terms of the older person's strengths, desires, capabilities and available resources, and to develop and implement an appropriate intervention plan.

Implementation and follow-up are particularly important. The assessment is rarely a one-off exercise and usually requires on-going negotiation and adjustment by the older person, the family and the mediator to changing needs and shifts in available resources. Agreements and implementation plans need to be regularly reviewed in the light of changing needs and circumstances.

Adult–elder mediation is increasingly being used in situations where an older family member is diagnosed with dementia. The condition, for which there is no known cure or medical treatment, results in the gradual deterioration of memory, intellect and the ability for self-care. Its onset is slow and insidious and leads to major personality alteration, markedly affecting the individual's ability to continue to relate to the world around them. It is a condition that presents a social problem of considerable magnitude in countries with an ageing demographic. It is difficult to diagnose and is a major challenge in terms of its biopsycho-social management over often quite long periods of time. In the early phase of mild dementia, the older person usually has some degree of awareness of cognitive deficits and is attempting to compensate and struggle to maintain a level of social functioning. Dementia may or may not be diagnosed at this time.

The initial task of a mediator who comes in contact with a family where dementia is suspected is be to help them to locate a general practitioner, geriatrician or psychogeriatrician who is accessible and knowledgeable about the condition, and able to make an appropriate assessment and exclude other possible causes related to depression, drugs, malnutrition and infection. At this stage, a thorough interdisciplinary assessment should be undertaken, including neuro-psychological testing. It is important that current behaviour be assessed in the light of past life patterns, behaviour, the quality of relationships and family interaction. If a diagnosis has not been obtained, one of the initial tasks of mediation might be to assist a family with this and in negotiating the various tests that may be necessary to confirm a diagnosis. Even gaining access and engagement requires specific skills, as many families are suspicious and anxious about seeking outside help with what appear to be relationship problems.

Mediation tasks involve assisting the family to access appropriate information about dementia and its probable course. Using a therapeutic model the mediator supports the older person and family members through the shock, confusion, fear and denial associated with loss and grief. The storytelling stage of the mediation is particularly important. The mediator assists the older person and family members to plan for the future while acknowledging the variability in the progress of the condition. Intervention at this relatively early phase should capitalise on the older person's remaining capacities to reflect on his or her situation and build in maximum support to maintain social interaction. It will require adjustments within the family, in terms of expectations and demands due to changed capacities of the person with dementia. It is also important for the older person and family members at this stage, while the judgements of the older person are not too confused, to make business and legal decisions that will affect the future. This can be an area of conflict, as family members may not agree who should assist in managing the older person's affairs. Disputes over claims to future inheritance can cloud decision making about the care of the older person and can impact negatively upon the care provided and ongoing relationships.

You are referred an adult–elder mediation after an older family member has been hospitalised following a fall. While in hospital, he has been diagnosed with mild dementia. His daughter has contacted the hospital saying she is concerned that her father is no longer able to manage at home on his own and should be put in residential care. He lives on his own in the country. There are two other daughters and a son in the family. When you suggest having a family meeting to discuss her father's needs, interests and concerns, she tells you not to worry about contacting any of the other family members. She informs you one of her sisters is living interstate and is mentally unstable and has not provided any care for her father over the years. She advises that her brother has no contact and prefers this to continue. The other sister she describes as 'difficult' and it is probably best not to involve her as she will aggravate the situation.

Who do you invite to attend the elder-adult mediation session?

Workplace mediation

Settlement mediation is often used in workplace disputes. As discussed in chapter 3, the main objective is to encourage incremental bargaining in an endeavour to reach a compromise at a mid-point to the demands of both parties. The dispute is defined in terms of the parties' definitions of the problem and their positions.[23] Main areas of conflict are over pay and conditions of employment, occupational heath and safety, workplace relations and unfair dismissal.

The use of advocates is common in workplace disputes.[24] Advocacy requires a strong ethical basis. At the heart of advocacy are the rights to humane treatment and participation in society on equal terms. A person may decide to bring in an advocate, or a mediator may suggest it. A mediator may assess that a person requires an advocate or support person to assist them to participate as fully and equally as possible in the mediation process. Mediators are required to analyse the conflict according to issues of power arising from class, race, ethnicity and culture age, gender, disability, sexuality and spirituality.[25] An advocate who is a legal representative may result in one party being in a more powerful position. This raises the issues of costs and also the dangers of introducing adversarial behaviours into the mediation process. The role of advocates is a crucial consideration and needs to be addressed and agreed upon before the commencement of the mediation.

Ross is a thirty-year-old male middle manager, who was accused of sexually harassing a young woman, Sinead aged twenty-three years, who was on four-week trial employment with the company as his personal assistant. She complained to the manager of the company that Ross tried to kiss her one night when you were both working back late together. When she rejected his advances and shouted at him angrily, he laughed and told her he had all night and to stop playing hard to get. She said he blocked her path as she ran for the door and had to struggle to get past him.

Ross denies these accusations vehemently but wants to settle the matter quickly and quietly in a confidential settlement. He does not want his wife to know about this in case she doesn't understand and leaves him and tries to take their two young children with her. Sinead really liked the job and hoped to be made permanent after the trial employment period. She was not kept on after the trial employment and believed it was due to her complaining about the incident with Ross. She tells the mediator privately that she wants $500,000 in compensation.

The manager of the company attends the mediation as Ross's support person and advocate. He does not want this matter to go any further and does not want it to harm the reputation of the company. The manager denies any claims of unfair dismissal and argues Sinead's work was unsatisfactory and that she was employed on a trial basis for four weeks only. The manager has told the mediator privately that to put an end to this matter he is prepared to pay Sinead $10,000.

Sinead takes her sister Margaret with her to the mediation as an advocate and support person. Margaret is angry because her sister Sinead has been unemployed for a long time. This job meant a lot to her and was her big chance of a career. Margaret lives with Sinead and they both struggle to pay the bills. Margaret wants Ross to pay for what he did to Sinead. Margaret tells the mediator in private that she thinks it is terribly unfair that Ross keeps his job after what happened and that Sinead, the innocent party, has lost her job and future work opportunities as a result. Margaret tells the mediator that she knows Sinead wants $500,000 in compensation but thinks perhaps this is a bit high.

1. *What role do you think the advocates should play in this mediation?*
2. *Is it appropriate to reach a confidential settlement in a conflict that involves accusations of sexual harassment?*
3. *As mediator, how would you ensure a fair and equitable outcome?*

Criminal justice

Restorative justice

Restorative justice is concerned with repairing the harm caused by offending that involves the offender, the victim, family members and significant others as well as any other parties with a direct interest in the process. Restorative justice developed within the context of increased dissatisfaction of victims in criminal justice systems and processes that were seen to neglect and silence the voice of victims. A prominent victim's rights advocate in the mid-1970s, Nils Christie, a professor of criminology from Oslo, conceptualised 'conflict as property'. He argued that the parties directly involved in a conflict had been removed (victims in particular) and that conflict had become the property of state authorised professionals including police, lawyers and administrators who are involved in what he terms 'professional manipulation'. He applies the concept of 'segmentation' to highlight the depersonalised social structures that make it difficult to evaluate the performance of these professionals who are generally referred to in terms of their different roles not as people. For Christie, further segmentation occurs through a system which is characterised by segmentation according to biological markers of race, sex, age and disability. He argues that this grouping and segregation leads to depersonalisation. The grouping of young people for instance shows higher representation in prison populations, high levels of unemployment and dependence on welfare, and what Christie refers to as 'educational incarceration' as young people are being encouraged to enter and stay in higher education for extended periods accruing debt, often without improvements in employment prospects. He considers the privatisation of disputes and confidential processes that involve few people and weaker parties are open to abusive practices. He argues that visibility is important for effective conflict management that involves the parties directly affected by the conflict with the victim/s provided the opportunity to describe how they have been affected and for the offender to listen, explain himself and be actively involved creating the possibility of forgiveness. For Christie, this is a likely preferred outcome for the offender when compared with the humiliation of the offender that occurs in regular court processes.[26]

Restorative justice is used in a range of different models that share the same basic principles of: (1) being future focused; (2) involving the victim and the offender, (3) restoration and (4) community integration. This is based on the premise that crime originates from social conditions and relationships within the community and that the community has some responsibility to ameliorate social conditions conducive to crime. A central premise is that the parties directly involved must be involved in developing solutions. This requires flexibility and agility within the justice system to be able to respond appropriately to the unique needs and contexts of different circumstances.

Conferencing

Mediation in criminal proceedings in the justice area is based upon restorative justice principles. Conferencing was originally used for less serious offences, and this continues to be the case for juvenile offenders. However, it is now used for more serious offences of assault, arson and homicide for adult offenders. An admission of guilt by the accused is required for participation in a conference. The aim is to improve the satisfaction of victims with the criminal justice system, increase the awareness of offenders of the impacts of their behaviour on others and to promote reparation to victims (direct or indirect), promote the rehabilitation and community integration of young offenders, and instil community confidence in the justice system. It is commonly referred to as family group conferencing, family group cautioning conference, youth conferencing, victim/offender mediation, re-integrative shaming or circle sentencing. The aim is to have a meeting between a person who has made an admission of committing an offence in the presence of family members, with the victim of the offence and the mediator. In some instances, respected members of the community conduct the mediation session.

Conferencing is used in all criminal justice jurisdictions in varying degrees and models for both juvenile and adult offences, although it is mostly used with young people. It is complementary to conventional criminal justice systems rather than replacing these. The pathway through the juvenile system for young offenders is arrest, police caution, probation, youth supervision order, attendance order and lastly custody in a youth training centre. In the state of Victoria, referrals for youth conferencing are made by the Children's Court. To be eligible for a referral to a youth conference, a young person must have admitted guilt or been found to be guilty of lesser offences that do not include sexual offences, manslaughter or homicide. The offence needs to be considered serious enough to warrant orders for probation, supervision or detention in a youth detention centre. The young person needs to be assessed by a government representative as suitable for a youth conference and the young person must consent to participation. In the juvenile justice area, conference facilitators are often police. Conferencing is used for diversion, to determine a sentence, as a sentencing and post-release.

In conferencing in youth justice settings, mediators require comprehensive knowledge of how technology and artificial intelligence is used in law enforcement for the apprehension of the young person, sentencing decisions and alternative pathways. This requires a broad understanding of the role of technology in law enforcement and how technology and artificial intelligence are used to both detect and commit crimes. This includes the development of new technology enabled sanctions for monitoring people as alternatives to community corrections orders, youth detention and prison.

Restorative justice conferencing models

Family group conferencing

Family group conferencing requires an admission of guilt and restoration to the victim.[27] 'Reintegrative shaming' is often used to denounce the offender's actions and integrate them back into the community. Parties include the offender, the victim and friends and family of both the victims and offenders. The purpose is to reveal the impacts on those affected by the crime. All of the parties present are involved in deciding what reparations are most appropriate.[28] It is argued that rather than shaming the focus should be on regret. This is due to the dangers and demoralising effects of shaming on the individual psyche; this is particularly damaging for young people whose brains are still developing. This approach has no evidence-base and is not to be condoned under any circumstances, particularly given the association between shame and suicide. What is important is regret and it is important to distinguish this from shame. Research evidence has shown improved outcomes when regret is evident and not shame.[29]

Victim–offender mediation

Victim–offender mediation also requires an admission of guilt and is focused on the needs of the victim, and the involvement and protection of the victim. These sessions are run by trained mediators who facilitate a process whereby offenders and victims meet in a structured and safe environment to discuss the harms inflicted with the offender held directly accountable for their behaviour. Outcomes are reached between the victim and the offender as to how the harm can be repaired.

A police-run victim–offender mediation model was established in Wagga Wagga by the New South Wales police in a pilot scheme between 1991 and 1994.[30] A number of police-run schemes based on this model are now operating throughout other parts of New South Wales, the Northern Territory Queensland, the Australian Capital Territory and Tasmania. All of these police-run mediation schemes are based upon the Wagga Wagga model of what has also been called 'effective cautioning'; a police caution. The police conduct the mediation and are responsible for organising it and deciding who should attend. Parties include the victim, victim support persons, offender and the offender's family and significant others. The acknowledgement of regret for the offence by the offender, and the development of empathy between the victim and the offender are central. The aim is for the offender to accept responsibility for the offending behaviour and to make amends. Acceptance of the young person back into the community of peers or relatives is a key feature; the offending behaviour is acknowledged as part of a community problem rather than due to the character of the offender. Parties in attendance include the offender, his or her family and support person, the victim or victim representative, and a police youth aid officer or the arresting police. The involvement of the victim or victim representative is crucial to this model as it confronts offenders with the consequences of their actions and encourages them to empathise with their victims.[31] A focus is on rehabilitation of the offender and reintegration into the community. The conference is finalised when agreement is reached between the victim, the offender and the police. If there is no agreement or admission to the offence by the person, the matter is referred to the court for determination. The agreed outcomes are recorded and are enforceable by the courts.

A further model developed in different parts of New South Wales and Victoria focuses upon issues of empowerment of the offender, the offender's family and the victim to deal more effectively with the offending behaviour. Police do not play a major role in this model. Legal representation is built into this Victorian model whereas it is not a feature of the Wagga Wagga model. Evaluation outcomes of both the Wagga model and Victorian models indicate that they are both effective in deterring young people from re-offending.

Circle sentencing

Circle sentencing in the justice area originated with the Maori community in New Zealand. This model was strongly embedded in traditional Maori cultural values and traditions and the notion of community. These mediations are often conducted by a Maori community leader who is a justice coordinator from the Justice Department. Circle sentencing (also known as peace-making circles) are now widely used with Aboriginal and Torres Strait Islander communities in Australia and run by Aboriginal elders. Reintegration into the family and community and acceptance by cultural peers and elders is central to circle sentencing. This is a very respectful space and process with a circle of people who are concerned for each other and the entire community. Participants 'speak from the heart' and healing for all involved moving forwards.[32] A focus is on the input of community and the sharing of power and decision-making within the community and culturally appropriate solutions to make amends to the victim and community for healing to occur and to prevent future offending.

1. *What are the main issues that arise in the application of these different models?*
2. *Given that mediators are meant to be 'neutral third parties' how appropriate it is it for police to conduct such mediation sessions? List arguments in favour and arguments against.*
3. *Which model do you prefer and why?*

Three critical issues that arise in the application of these different models are power imbalances, coercive versus voluntary participation, net-widening and labelling. Often there are considerable power imbalances, particularly when the police are conducting the mediation with a young person. Clearly, they have power over what charges might be laid and whether or not they are pursued. As mediators, the police also have responsibility for preparing the agreement stating how the offender will make amends to the victim. The offender has little choice but to participate, because refusal could mean police charges and a court appearance. Since the introduction of mediation in criminal matters, an increasing number of young people are attending cautioning conferences who in the past would have simply received a police caution. These people are seen by others in the community to have offended and can be judged and labelled as offenders or criminals as a result. This can curtail opportunities, particularly those of leadership and responsibility. They may also be threatened with a harsher penalty if they do not participate.

Jason was fifteen years of age and charged by the New South Wales police for assaulting a policeman. Jason had been walking home one evening with a group of friends when they were stopped by the police. The police asked them where they were going and what they were doing out at that time. According to Jason, one of the police started to taunt him about his African features and gave him a push. Jason responded by pushing the police officer. Jason, who had not been in trouble with the police previously, now faced the serious charge of assaulting police. The police invited Jason and his family to attend a family group-cautioning conference. Jason and his family were concerned about the role of the police running the Conference and they feared that Jason would not receive a fair hearing. They were also concerned about the lack of legal representation. They were angry about the manner in which Jason had been treated by the police on the night of the assault and wanted to lay counter-charges of police assault on Jason.

The family worried that Jason's basketball coach would find out and that he would be removed as team captain and no longer allowed to coach the junior teams. His family decided not to attend the conference and instead hired a lawyer who negotiated with the police to have the charges dropped.

What possible outcomes might have resulted if Jason had attended the family group-cautioning conference?

David was sixteen years of age and was out with a friend one night when they decided to steal a car. They were caught by the police and admitted to having stolen the car as well as driving without a licence and being under-age. A family group conference was arranged whereby David and his friend came face to face with the man whose car they had stolen. They heard about his annoyance and the inconvenience he had been caused by having his car stolen. David and his friend offered to make amends by coming to his house each week for the next three months to wash his car. While the mediator seemed to think this was a fair outcome, the victim was not impressed and did not want David or his friend anywhere near his house or his car. He thanked them for the offer but declined to have any further contact with them.

Is it reasonable to expect victims to want to have further contact with offenders?

What issues may arise?

How can amends be made in ways that do not directly involve victims?

Therapeutic jurisprudence

Since the 1990s, we have seen the establishment of specialist courts underpinned by the principles of therapeutic jurisprudence and restorative justice for criminal proceedings. Therapeutic jurisprudence refers to legal processes and initiatives engaged in by Courts aimed at the rehabilitation of the offender by addressing underlying individual needs and social problems, such as substance misuse, that are considered to have contributed to the offending behaviour. It introduces notions of healing and concerns for well-being to legal processes and has a transformative and therapeutic focus unbderpinned by notions of natural justice.

A number of specialist courts have been developed in different jurisdictions and are also known as problem-solving courts or collaborative justice. In the state of Victoria, these specialist courts come under the Magistrates Court and include the Koori Court (operating in twelve metropolitan, regional and rural areas) and the Drug Court. Other jurisdictions, especially in the United States, also have specialist mental health courts. In the Koorie Court, the offender, family members and a legal team sit around a bench table with the magistrate, a Koorie Court officer, Aboriginal elders, and possibly Koorie-controlled agency representatives. The aim is to have a 'yarn' using plain language, avoiding legal terms and jargon, to inform the determination of a response that is culturally appropriate and likely to reduce recidivism. The Drug Court determines and administers Drug Treatment Orders (DTO). This includes a custodial community sentence of no more than two years and a requirement of supervision and treatment while on the DTO. People on DTOs are required to participate in regular follow-up with the Drug Court, participate in substance misuse rehabilitation, undergo routine substance use testing, engage in education and employment programs and abide by other conditions of the DTO that might include place of residence and a nightly curfew. The advantages of these specialist courts are that a conciliatory approach is used that includes treatment and follow-up rather than simply a punitive sentence. It holds professionals accountable for the provision of their services as well as clear responsibilities of the offender and court officers.

Neighbourhood disputes

Due to ongoing relationships in neighbourhood disputes, narrative, transformative and evaluative mediation models are particularly suited. A key consideration in mediation of neighbourhood and planning disputes is community standards and expectations. These will differ from one area to another and also will be influenced by age, culture and socio-economic background. In metropolitan areas in Australia there is an increase in medium- to high-density housing that means that people are living in closer proximity. However, in terms of privacy and noise, often old standards are applied. For instance, is it reasonable to expect not to hear your neighbours or not have any overlooking from neighbours' properties in medium to high-density living?

Neighbourhood disputes often arise over individual behaviour that is not acceptable to neighbours or other members of the community. Disputes over fences include whether or not a fence is needed, the type and height of the fence, who gets the smooth side and who is at fault if the fence collapses. Trees, shrubs and creepers are also a source of conflict particularly overhanging branches, overshadowing, encroaching vines and out of control creepers and tree roots lifting paving. Shared property can also cause tension such as right of use to shared driveways, gardens and roads. This is an increasing area of conflict since the increase in housing estates with shared facilities managed by a body corporate.

Behaviour of both adults and children can result in conflict between neighbours. Adult behaviour includes gossiping, making threats, graffiti and throwing rubbish into neighbours' gardens. Conflict involving children often involves children trampling on gardens to retrieve balls, children playing loudly, noisy teenage street and park gatherings, and abuse and insults. Noise is a particular source of aggravation between neighbours. This may be loud music, talking and laughter at an unacceptable hour, and, for those living in multi-storey accommodation, overhead noise such as dancing on floorboards. Neighbours also complain about noise from pool pumps and, of course, noise from animals, including barking, aggressive or untrained dogs.

Trevor ran a panel beating and spray painting business in his garage and driveway that bordered his neighbour Cleo's side fence. On the other side of the fence adjacent to where Trevor did his work was Cleo's daughter's bedroom window and the backyard swimming pool. Her daughter was constantly disturbed by the noise and paint fumes. On a windy day, paint spray was blown over the fence into the pool area. Cleo raised these concerns with Trevor, who denied that he was running a business and said that he was fixing his own car. Cleo complained to the council and was told she needed to record all of the offending activities for one month, including the time of day or night and duration, before the council would respond to her complaint. Cleo did so. Trevor was contacted by the council and denied the activities claimed by Cleo, saying that she was a troublemaker and had fabricated the record. The activity continued and Cleo eventually moved house to get away from Trevor.

1. *How can a mediator know what is really happening when each party tells a different version of events?*
2. *How could the conflict between Trevor and Cleo be managed more amicably?*

Property damage caused during construction and renovation can result in conflict between neighbours. This includes both accidental and malicious damage. Problems between neighbours also arise over water and drainage, with broken drains causing flooding or water running onto a neighbour's property. This is naturally less common in drought conditions. A neighbour's car parked outside the house can cause conflict, particularly if it is opposite a driveway or if it is a large truck or work vehicle. This is an increasing problem as companies allow workers to take trucks home overnight as a fringe benefit. While the worker may save on fuel costs and time in having to collect the truck from the depot, companies obtain most benefits by not having to store vehicles, and by reductions in vandalism. What it does mean is that you may end up with a Jim's Bins truck parked outside your house most evenings and weekends.

Pollution is another source of conflict, particularly smoke from wood heaters, and odours are also a cause of complaint.[33]

When Kiah and Rohit purchased their first home, the agent told them what a lovely older couple they had as neighbours. However, within a couple of days of having moved in, the older neighbour, Akiko, came to the door asking for an apple tree that was close to their fence to be cut down as the leaves were falling into her garden and blowing into her gutters. Kiah and Rohit were reluctant to cut the tree down but thought they'd be good neighbours and did as she requested. A couple of week's later, Akiko came to the door again, requesting a second apple tree be cut down. Again Kiah and Rohit preferred to keep the tree but cut it down to please her. This left them with two more apple trees as well as a large plum tree in the backyard. Akiko then requested both of the remaining apple trees be cut down. Kiah did not want to cut the trees down but Rohit agreed to do so. This left only the plum tree.

Akiko returned and insisted that the plum tree be cut down as well. She worried that it would fall on her house in a storm and complained that the leaves made a mess of her garden and blocked her spouting. Kiah told her she liked the tree and had no intention of cutting it down. She also pointed out that the tree was quite old and wondered why she had waited until they had moved in to insist all the trees be removed. Kiah, who was of Fijian background felt that the neighbour, who was of Japanese background, was acting in a racially superior way and expected them to follow her orders. When Kiah refused this request, Akiko said she would send her the bill for having her gutters cleared, including additional costs for damages.

The next day, Akiko's daughter came to Kiah's door and started swearing and shouting at her. She accused her of upsetting Akiko and causing her to have developed cancer. She said if Kiah refused to have the tree cut down, she would complain to the council. She handed Kiah the number of someone she recommended to remove the tree. When Kiah asked the daughter if her parents were prepared to contribute towards the cost of removing the tree, she swore once more, saying they were on a pension and could not afford to pay even if they wanted to.

The next week, Akiko came over, again insisting the tree be cut down. She also told Kiah she was worried that Kiah and Rohit's dog would jump the fence and attack her when she was putting out her washing and that she wanted them to get rid of it. Again Kiah refused these requests.

A few days later, Kiah opened the front door and found a pig's head on the doorstep. She called the police, who referred her to a neighbourhood dispute settlement centre.

1. *Who should be involved in this mediation?*
2. *What are the main needs, concerns and fears of the parties known so far?*
3. *What appear to be the main issues in this dispute?*
4. *What additional information may be required for the parties to reach agreement?*

Planning: conciliation

Main areas of conflict in planning disputes are home extensions that are considered to be an eyesore, overlooking and over-development. In planning disputes, the planner is often asked to assume the role of mediator. This can be problematic for two main reasons. Firstly, as an employee of the council, the planner is not a neutral third party and the planner possesses professional expertise that the parties expect to be shared. A planner who assumes the role of mediator and refuses to provide expert knowledge, claiming to be a neutral third party, is not likely to succeed at reaching an amicable agreement with the disputing parties.[34] In such circumstances, parties are likely to have little trust in the planner as mediator, or in the process. A preferred option is for councils to employ independent third-party mediators or to ask members to conduct such sessions.[35] Again the independence of councillors may be questioned. However, councillors may be more readily accepted as mediators and seen as neutral in that they are elected to represent the interests of all members of their community. The issue of costs is often a prohibitive factor when employing outside mediators, particularly when it is the expectation that this is part of the planner's role. Developments within the planning profession have seen conflict management and mediation included as core curriculum in 36 qualifications.[36]

Planners are increasingly required to conduct public meetings as well as mediate disputes. Often, public meetings result in people having their say on an issue, with members of the audience taking sides for or against an issue. This is generally in relation to the development of a particular area. These meetings often degenerate into accusations and grandstanding, with people more concerned with having their say rather than listening to other views expressed.

A public meeting was held to consider a proposal for a nursing home development in a new subdivision. The meeting was advertised throughout the local area. As well as the time and venue, it was mentioned that there would be a presentation on what was to be included in the proposed development by the company who would be running the nursing home. This meeting was chaired by a local planner with approximately 100 people in attendance. A computer and projector were set up for a slide show of the development.

The meeting began with the planner introducing the nursing home developer, who proceeded to talk about his company and other nursing home developments they had undertaken. He had not spoken for long when members of the audience started jeering and heckling, telling him to get out and that his development was not wanted in this area. This met applause from some members of the audience. The planner asked members of the audience to listen to the developer and let him have his say. This was met with further calls for him and his company to get out, with one man saying aggressively, 'You just don't get it, do you? We don't want to know about the development because we don't want it.' This met with further applause and laughter.

Again, the planner called the meeting to order. A young woman in the audience called out, saying that she wanted to hear about the proposed development and that was why she had come to the meeting. The developer then started to describe the proposed development further. He had not spoken for long when a man in the audience who lived opposite the proposed development spoke of his concerns about the development, including increased traffic from staff cars coming and going at all hours as well as ambulances and hearses and lowering of property prices in the area. Other people also spoke up against the development. The local ward councillor who was sitting quietly in the audience stood up and introduced himself and said he wanted the community to know that he was listening to their concerns. Another man spoke, saying that he had nothing against the development but that it was not the right location. He suggested another location a few blocks away. This aroused the concern of members of the meeting who lived in the other proposed location.

The meeting continued for two hours, with people shouting out and interjecting and the developer not getting past the first slide in his presentation. The planner sat quietly for most of the time.

At the end of the meeting, a member of the audience asked the developer if he planned to proceed with the nursing home. He replied that it was not likely, due to the amount of feeling expressed against the development by the local community. He later withdrew his application and the development did not proceed. In the meantime, the councillor at the meeting sent a letter to all local residents to say that he would work to prevent the proposed nursing home development going ahead.

1. *How successful was this meeting?*
2. *Is it appropriate for public meetings to be conducted in this manner as a forum for people to have their say?*
3. *How might the planner have conducted this meeting more effectively?*

Perceptions of possible bias are important and must be responded to appropriately for conflict management to succeed. A preferred model of dispute management for planners is to have two conciliators: one who acts impartially and manages the process, while the other providing expert advice and information.[37] Often the two are seated at opposite ends of a table to clearly distinguish the different roles they are performing. Again this requires appropriate resource allocation by councils by committing two planners to the conflict management process. Due to the expert advisory role performed in such sessions, it is more accurate to call this conciliation rather than mediation.[38] This allows the planners to provide information and make suggestions and recommendations that would not normally be made in mediation. Often when large numbers of people are involved, a spokesperson is nominated for each party.

A property developer plans to build eight units on a block of land in a quiet court location. Residents in adjoining properties and the rest of the court have drawn up a petition to the council to try and stop the development going ahead. They have expressed concerns about the extra traffic and noise in their quiet street and are worried about young children being run over. The residents are angry about the proposed development and believe it should not go ahead. They have also complained that the design of the units is not in keeping with the quality of other properties in the court. They argue that these cheap units will bring down the property values of neighbouring homes. The situation has been referred to the planner at the council in an attempt to resolve the dispute.

1. *What parties you will include in the conciliation and in what role/s?*
2. *Where will you conduct the conciliation?*
3. *You have a neighbourhood activist who does not live in the court but who is concerned about the increase in medium-density housing in the local area. He contacts council to say he wants to attend the session. What do you do? Do you include him? If yes, in what role?*
4. *What additional information may be needed to effectively resolve this dispute?*

Conclusion

Mediation has been conducted informally in many cultures for centuries. However, since the late twentieth century there has been an increase in requirements for formal education and training to practise in this area. This has occurred alongside greater use of mandatory mediation in some jurisdictions, particularly family law. Different dispute resolution processes, and models of mediation are more suited to different practice contexts. Models particularly suited to family conflict, including parent–adolescent and adult–elder disputes, are therapeutic, narrative, transformative and evaluative mediation. Collaborative family law is also used by lawyers mediating family disputes using an assisted negotiation process. In parent–adolescent mediation, a peer mediation model is often used with a young person and an adult co-mediating. A main focus is on engaging the adolescent in the mediation process. There is an increasing demand for adult–elder mediation, particularly in relation to issues of care. Advocacy can be a key feature of adult–elder mediation to ensure that the mediation focuses on the best interests of the older person. Advocacy is also central to workplace disputes; settlement mediation is often used as a preferred model. Mediation in the justice area is commonly referred to as family group conferencing, family group cautioning conference, victim/offender mediation or re-integrative shaming. A focus is on rehabilitation of the offender and reintegration into the community. It is argued that re-integrative shaming is demoralising and particularly damaging for young people and not to be condoned under any circumstances. Neighbourhood disputes focus on managing the current dispute, with a focus on ongoing future relationships. Due to these ongoing relationships narrative, transformative and evaluative mediation models are particularly suited. In planning disputes, conciliation is the preferred process rather than mediation. This is due to conciliation acknowledging the expertise of the planner in terms of advisory role as well as process management.

In the next chapter, complex environmental and multiparty disputes are considered alongside a model of policy-making mediation.

8

Complex Multiparty Disputes: Policy-making Mediation

Policy-making mediation is a useful strategy for preventing conflict, as well as problem-solving and ongoing conflict management in complex environments. Policy-making mediation is well suited to international conflicts, including issues of economic development and environmental and social sustainability. Policy-making mediation, particularly in an international context, may seem quite daunting and a major leap from mediating disputes between neighbours or co-workers. It is necessarily more complex due to the policy focus and trans-boundary issues. However, the problem-defining and problem-solving phases are essentially the same.

Policy-making mediation is a process by which agreements reached during mediation are enacted in the development of policies, standards, procedures and regulations. It is often used for developing environmental standards, because it is valuable for exploring the nature and causes of conflicts in the environment, and identifying interests and priorities.

This chapter explores the main features of policy-making mediation. Policy-making mediation is suited to all disputes requiring the development and implementation of policy with the focus of this chapter on its application to environmental and international conflicts. A case study of policy-making mediation in the Mekong River Basin is presented.

Policy-making mediation

Governments are increasingly restructuring legislation and regulatory procedures to include more conciliatory processes for conflict management.[1] Debates about the suitability of mediation for handling complex multi-party disputes are wide-ranging. Even where it is agreed that mediation is appropriate, disputes occur over the most suitable models of mediation, and who is best to provide them. There is considerable support for mediation as a preferred strategy to prevent environmental disputes and to establish policies and strategies for effective conflict management.[2] As Elix suggests, though, the categorising of such disputes can be problematic: 'Environmental conflict or dispute is a misnomer. These are in reality social conflicts between those advocating the interests of various groups of people with a concern related to the environment and economic interests needing to be taken into account.'[3]

Due to the complexity of the issues and the multitude of parties involved, disputes related to the environment are often intractable. The disputes often transcend jurisdictional and ministerial portfolio boundaries both nationally and internationally. Issues frequently involve water, land and natural resources. Strong emotions arise over rights of ownership and use, including fears for the future loss of species, pollution, degradation and sustainability for current and future generations.[4] Governments often defer decision making, fearing loss of votes from decisions that marginalise such significant interest groups as industry or farmers. Often due to the incompatibility of values and interests, it is simply not possible to reach a consensus. And even where agreement is reached, it is often 'arrived at on the lowest common denominator'.[5]

An effective policy-making mediation results in a negotiated agreement that seeks to maximise joint gains for all parties involved. The process facilitates the strengthening of relationships for future conflict prevention and management, and sustainable development. The goal of sustainable development is harmony between environmental protection and economic development by using natural resources in a manner that enables indefinite use.[6] Activities aimed at economic growth are to be conducted so as not to cause social or political disruption or deplete natural resources.[7] In this way, a sustainable society or region 'continues generation after generation, neither depleting its resource base by exceeding sustainable yields nor producing pollutants in excess of nature's capacity to absorb them'.[8] This conveys that conflict management processes remain in place for exploration and reflection on sustainable development and practices, and that the enforcement of agreements is a main focus of policy-making mediation. Policy-making mediation is particularly suited to environmental and international disputes.

Environmental conflict

Environmental conflict is generally caused by competing demands for scarce natural resources.[9] This is particularly evident in the use and allocation of depleted natural resources and the reciprocal impacts of land and water uses. Conflict often occurs due to inadequate governance arrangements, disagreement over data and different interests and priorities. Structural differences can result in power imbalances that lead to high levels of mistrust in relationships. Environmental disputes often involve large numbers of people. Strategies are required to locate spokespersons who can participate in the mediation and represent the interests of main groups in the conflict.

A multinational company, ALSO, is planning to start coal mining activities and build a power station in Seahaven, a small coastal community. The company is keen for the development to proceed but is concerned that complaints from environmental and local Indigenous groups may prevent it. The project manager wants the development to proceed smoothly with as little disruption as possible. He has organised an environmental impact assessment report on the site and argues that there are no health risks to the local population. ALSO plans to invest in the local community and will contribute to the infrastructure of the town in terms of sustainable community initiatives. These include investing in local schools, youth and family services, hospitals, aged care and tourism – including tours of the proposed green star design power station.

The council is very keen for the development to proceed because of the investment in the local community that the company will provide. The mine and power plant will provide a boost for an economy that is experiencing high levels of unemployment. The mayor has worked at attracting the company to the area and is keen for the development to proceed while also ensuring that health and safety regulations are complied with.

A number of groups are opposed to the mine. The Seahaven Environmental Group is very concerned about the environmental impacts of the proposed development. They are particularly worried about hazardous emissions from the proposed site, and odour and waste disposal into the sea. They are also worried about impacts on local vegetation and wildlife. The shoreline is a muttonbird roosting area, and the environmental group are worried that the development will interfere with this. They are also concerned about the delicate ecosystem in the area and do not want it disturbed. Group members are very excited about recent sightings of the yellow-bellied thrush, an endangered species native to the area, whose numbers have been dwindling in recent years. The opponents of the plan see the proposed development as an environmental disaster for the area and are vehemently opposed to it. Members of the Nora Nora Indigenous Group are opposed to the development on the grounds that the proposed area is a sacred site based on a significant rock formation. Before white settlement, Seahaven was called Nora Nora and was a popular fishing area for the Nora Nora tribe. Natural Landscape Australia is a group that opposes mining developments and forestry, and has a particular dislike for large multinational companies. The group views these companies as destroying the natural landscape and buying off local communities with little concern for any long-term investment or development. Two years ago, the group stopped ALSO from proceeding with a similar proposed development in another town.

The local council has employed a team of mediators to resolve this conflict. ALSO has generously provided the council with the funds to cover the cost of the mediation.

1. *What are the power issues in this conflict?*
2. *What are the environmental, social and economic issues? Are they compatible?*
3. *What ethical issues are present?*
4. *What might the mediation goal be?*
5. *Who would you include in the mediation?*

6. *Where would you conduct the mediation?*
7. *Is a win/win outcome possible?*
8. *What might an enforceable agreement look like?*

Policy-making mediation in the Mekong River Basin[10]

Neighbouring countries that have one-third of the world's population share one river, the Mekong. The Mekong River commences in Yunnan province in China and flows through eastern Myanmar (Burma), Thailand, Lao PDR, Cambodia and Vietnam. From its source in China to Vietnam and the South China Sea, the Greater Mekong River basin encompasses an expansive network of waterways covering an area of approximately 795,000 square kilometres.[11] Large populations in each of these countries depend upon the river and its tributaries for their sustenance and livelihood; the well-being of these nations is closely linked to the river. The Mekong River Basin is a delicate ecosystem rich in natural resources and biodiversity. Over the centuries, the countries in the basin have shared the resources of this mighty river. However, increasingly, concerns have been raised about overuse and the health of the river and how it is to be shared among neighbouring nations and those whose lives depend on it. Concerns have been brought about by increases in population, altering the rivers natural flow and course through dams and waterways, increased industrialisation and tourism and changes to traditional land and water use.

The Mekong region

The Mekong River Basin is the eighth-largest in the world in terms of annual discharge. The wet season flow results in the inundation of one to four million hectares of riverine forest, wetland and agricultural areas for up to four metres for two to five months annually.[12] By depositing silt and irrigating land, retreating flood waters provide the basis for traditional agricultural practices. Flooded areas also serve as hatcheries for one of the most productive fresh water fisheries in the world. The regions biodiversity is among the richest in the world but is being seriously threatened. The natural flooding system is in danger primarily because of the construction of dams in the upper reaches of the Mekong. The extensive construction of dams and reservoirs would change the water regime of the river, increasing dry season flows and reducing wet season flows. A constant flow would significantly affect flooding and natural fish spawning, lead to an increase in irrigated agriculture and the further loss of flood plains and natural wetlands.

Large areas of flooded forest are being cleared for agriculture with serious implications for fish spawning. Approximately half of the forests of the lower basin have been cleared in the past three decades. Human-induced hydrological changes are closely related to new farming practices. Agricultural production in the delta and the central highlands of Vietnam is being further transformed through intensification of farming practices, foreign investment and increased commercialisation. The protection of the region's natural resource base is essential for maintaining and improving the quality of life of the people who live in and rely on the basin for their sustenance and livelihood. The rate of deterioration of the biodiversity and natural resources in the region is of major concern. The increased decline of natural resources will necessarily impact upon local people by reducing the capacity of rural populations to sustain themselves. This is likely to lead to extensive migration to cities.

Lessons from other river basins

Human extraction and use of water from rivers is increasingly a source of tension, particularly when the rivers cross political boundaries. Water scarcity, water sharing, economic and environmental issues all contribute to the complexity of reaching cooperative arrangements within and between countries. Competing demands for water in river systems are creating increasing pressures resulting in a rising number of social, economic and environmental issues.

Dam building for irrigation and hydropower has been an important means of meeting water and energy services for economic growth.[13] However, negative impacts of dam building such as the fragmentation and transformation of the world's rivers, ecosystem destruction, debt burdens, population displacement and the inequitable sharing of costs and benefits, have led to serious questioning of the future of large dam building projects.[14] Livelihoods of people within river basins can be intricately linked to the availability of water resources, particularly in arid or semi-arid areas such as the Nile River Basin. The complexity of river basin management is heightened considerably in the case of trans-boundary water management issues.

Integrated river basin management is widely accepted as the best approach for management of freshwater resources.[15] Integrated river basin management must deal with a range of conflicting economic, social and environmental issues. Control of river resources is a basis for conflict, but driven by water quantity and/or water quality factors.[16] Regional instability is also a cause for concern in terms of the potential use of force over the sharing of riparian resources. Examples of historical and more recent conflict are provided by a number of river basins both within Australia and internationally. To better understand the causes of tension, and institutions and agreements in other regions, two case studies are explored briefly: the Nile River Basin and the Murray Darling Basin. Lessons to be learnt from these examples are drawn together to provide a basis for exploring the need for conflict management and effective mediation in the Mekong region.

The Nile River Basin

The Nile River flows through ten riparian nations. Almost all of the flow of the Nile is generated in an area covering approximately 20 per cent of the basin.[17] Egypt, Sudan, Rwanda and Uganda are almost completely dependent on the flow of the Nile for water. Ninety-seven per cent of Egypt's water and seventy-seven per cent of Sudan's water originates from outside the borders of those countries: Ethiopia supplies eighty-six per cent of the water to the Nile.[18] The 1959 bilateral agreement between Egypt and Sudan excluded Ethopia and brought considerable tension in the region.[19] In the 1970s, the Marxist regime of Ethiopia began studying the feasibility of damming tributaries of the

Nile. Egypt threatened to destroy any dams built with military force. In the early 1990s, further political conflict between Sudan and Egypt arose through the formation of a joint Blue Nile Valley organisation between Sudan and Ethiopia to explore major infrastructure projects. Egypt again responded with the threat of military action.[20] A decade later, the Nile River Basin Cooperative Framework was established to 'attain a regional cooperative framework acceptable to all basin countries in order to promote basin-wide cooperation in integrated water resources planning and management'.[21]

A shared vision was developed to 'achieve sustainable socio-economic development through the equitable utilisation of, and benefit from, the common Nile Basin water resources'.[22] An International Consortium for Cooperation on the Nile (ICCON) was been established as a forum for riparian nations and the international community to support sustainable development in the Nile River Basin. The first meeting of this consortium was held in 2001 in Geneva.[23] The World Bank, the United Nations and the Canadian International Development Agency and other international institutions have been seen as pivotal in developing the foundation of a multilateral platform for dialogue, as well as associated funding arrangements.[24] However, others in the region have been more sceptical of involvement of the international community. In 1999 the Sudanese Minister for Irrigation and Water Resources is reported as cautioning riparian nations to beware of interference by foreign powers in Nile water affairs and not to be deceived by 'some concepts, like water trade and water privatisation, promoted by Zionist circles to serve their ambitions in the Nile water'.[25]

In 2010, a cooperative framework agreement was signed by five upstream countries: Ethiopia, Kenya, Uganda, Rwanda and Tanzania, with Burundi signing in 2011, in an endeavour to obtain more water from the Nile. Upstream country representatives were reported as saying they were 'tired of first getting approval from Egypt before using Nile river water for irrigation and development projects'.[26] Egypt and Sudan were not signatories to this agreement.

A number of developments have occurred, but cooperation, water sharing and trans-boundary arrangements in the Nile River Basin are still at an early stage. So far, little has been achieved on reaching agreement about the sharing and management of the Nile Basin. Legislation, policies and rules of engagement to address trans-boundary issues are not evident, nor are processes for the prevention and management of conflict.[27] The wider context of distrust, internal and regional struggles and the political climate of the region may act as barriers to cooperative arrangements. However, the emergence of the Nile Basin initiative shows a trend globally towards negotiation and agreements in basin management.[28] The limitations recognise the need for a framework for negotiation, inclusive of all stakeholders, without which conflict is very likely to continue in the region in the face of growing pressure on the finite resource that the Nile offers.

The Murray Darling Basin

The Murray Darling Basin has had a substantially longer history of basin-wide management. It covers an area of over one million square kilometres in five states and territories, extending over much of the central and south eastern inland area of Australia. It contains twenty major river systems and twenty per cent of Australia's irrigated area.[29] The value of farm outputs is significant from the irrigated areas and from dry land areas. Major environmental problems have arisen from 150 years of agricultural practice. Extensive tree clearing, wetlands draining, water diversions and dam construction have led to serious threats to biological diversity and extensive salinisation of rivers, streams, wetlands and land. These environmental problems are now causing serious economic impacts.

Although the Murray Darling Basin is contained within one nation, it crosses state and territory boundaries. The Australian federal system of government under a constitution allocates powers between the Commonwealth government and the states and territories. States have full sovereign powers over land, water and natural resources. Intergovernmental arrangements between the Commonwealth, state and territory governments were first put in place for the Murray Darling area in 1982 through the Murray Darling Basin Agreement, which aimed to plan and manage the sustainable use of the region's resources in a cooperative and coordinated way. Initial partners were the Commonwealth, New South Wales, Victorian and South Australian governments. The agreement was rewritten in 1992 to include Queensland. The Australian Capital Territory was also later admitted as a non-voting member. The Murray Darling Basin Agreement informed the implementation of the *Murray Darling Basin Act 1993*. This Commonwealth legislation specified Heads of Powers between governments. For example, the agreement contains detailed water-sharing arrangements between the governments and provides the basis for works. It includes a cap on water extractions as a schedule under which governments agree to limit diversions. This Act has been replaced by the *Water Act 2007* (incorporating amendments 2013). The Water Act makes provision for the management of water resources in the Murray Darling Basin as well as provision for other matters related to water of a national interest.

A ministerial council was established in 1986 comprising the ministers of participating governments with land, water and environmental responsibilities. The council was the peak intergovernmental decision making authority. In 1988, the Murray Darling Basin Commission was established, incorporating the previous management authority for the Murray River. The commission comprised officials from government agencies and also included a secretariat of sixty persons based in Canberra. It provided executive support and advice to the Ministerial Council, implemented council decisions, developed policy, planning, management and works proposals, operated the river system by regulating flows and managed assets such as dams. The Murray Darling Basin Authority was established under the *Water Act 2007* and became the principal government agency to manage the Murray Darling Basin in an integrated and sustainable way.

These cooperative arrangements specify the rules of engagement between governments and allow them to implement decisions in their own way. For example, states manage their own water and land legislation and allocate water and land uses within the framework of the intergovernmental water sharing arrangements. The Murray Darling Authority has prepared a salinity and drainage strategy in an attempt to establish salinity targets for every major river. Tensions have arisen particularly when upstream activities impact negatively on those downstream. For example, the South Australian government has objected to continued broad-scale land clearing higher in the catchment in Queensland, and the increased salinity levels this clearing causes downstream. Increased salinity levels threaten to make the quality of water taken from the Murray River for Adelaide unsuitable for human consumption.[30]

Agreements on water sharing and placing a limit on water extractions are major achievements. However, intergovernmental arrangements have not successfully managed land and water use. Water has continued to be over allocated, with too little available for environmental purposes. Inappropriate land and water uses have continued. Decisions that radically alter current practice have been difficult to achieve. Following lengthy negotiations between the commonwealth and state governments and numerous submissions from stakeholders, the Basin Plan was legislated in 2012, to return water to the basin by cutting water entitlements.

The strengths of the Murray Darling arrangements are primarily gaining intergovernmental cooperation and commitment, and also mechanisms for integrating stakeholder participation and a solid understanding of the issues through increasingly better data.[31] Although hardly perfect, the Murray Darling Authority has a highly developed environmental mandate. Key lessons are inclusion of stakeholders, processes for policy and legislative formulation, adaptability in management, and cooperation in addressing the clash between production-oriented uses and environmental requirements.

Water sharing

In terms of factors contributing to conflict, possibly the most important is the inherent contradiction between the finite water available, and the use of water resources as a basis for economic growth and development. Unilateral actions resulting from self-interest and lack of cooperation, or exclusion of riparian nations from water-sharing arrangements have been the cause of conflict in a number of regions. The basic issue of sovereignty and how countries can meet their own demands and needs without harming or reducing opportunities for other nations is perhaps the most difficult issue to overcome. This raises the question of how to achieve a level of cooperation that includes all riparian nations, and integrate decision making in a way that is equitable and promotes development, as well as taking account of broader social and environmental issues.

A large number of international treaties for water sharing exist but most are inadequate containing no monitoring or enforcement mechanisms. They do not promote regional governance, and contain terms which are general and difficult to apply, and therefore have little impact.[32] The quality of treaties is crucial. The existence of a treaty aimed at cooperation is not sufficient to prevent conflict. Agreements need to be binding, with legislative support and an effective policy framework. Regional governance is required that considers transboundary issues and has a strong institutional framework specifying rules of engagement between nations. The means for prevention or management of conflict and a continuous process of implementation and re-examination of the performance of agreements is required.

Legal and policy responses

The United Nations 1997 Convention on the Law of Non-Navigational Uses of Watercourses is the basis of the international regulatory framework for international watercourses. The cornerstone of the convention are the principles of 'equitable reasonable utilisation' and 'no harm'. The convention reflects universal principles that can assist with negotiating and interpreting agreements. The application of these principles in workable transnational agreements has been questioned due to substantial divisions amongst nations and states.[33] However, others argue that the process of agreement and negotiation on international water resources is the only way forward if we are to avoid the predicted 'water wars' based on the Harmon Doctrine of absolute sovereignty.[34]

There is an extensive environmental legal framework in the countries of the Mekong River Basin and improved environmental laws are gradually being introduced. However, many laws are general and difficult to apply, and monitoring and enforcement are often weak. Policies are general statements applying rules, principles or procedures to individual cases over time, and are intended to assist consistent decision making by providing a context in which to assess individual cases and situations rather than incremental case by case decisions. The development, consistent application, monitoring and enforcement of policy is an effective way to avoid conflict. The absence of policy means that a reference point is lacking which could be otherwise used to prevent, manage or resolve conflict.

International environmental and resource management agreements come about from the acceptance by countries of the need for collective action to solve problems, the desire to prevent conflict over deteriorating or scarce resources, and the acceptance of the benefits which may accrue to countries through cooperation. However, there is usually tension between perceptions of national interest by signatory countries and the willingness to surrender national decision making to resolve common problems. This tension can lead to country disagreement and forms of conflict.[35]

The existence of treaties does not necessarily guarantee protection from conflict. The terms of many international agreements are inadequate to deal with increasing problems and rising tensions. Lack of clear laws, policies or definitive rules is common to intergovernmental agreements and organisations. No international environmental agreement includes effective enforcement mechanisms for non-compliance. Often, the agreement is an enabling document which allows participating countries to carry out measures voluntarily, or it provides directional statements that allow considerable discretion.

Multilateral treaties may also clash. For example, a number of multilateral agreements apply to the Mekong River. The Greater Mekong Subregion Initiative led by the Asian Development Bank proposes projects that would lead to environmental impacts or conflicts that the Mekong River Agreement was designed to prevent.[36]

The Mekong River Agreement and Mekong River Commission

In an endeavour to protect the Mekong River and promote sustainable development, the 1995 'Agreement on the Cooperation for the Sustainable Development of the Mekong River Basin', commonly known as the Mekong River Agreement was negotiated and signed by Thailand, Cambodia, Vietnam and Lao PDR, with China and Myanmar becoming dialogue partners in 2002. It is primarily a cooperative rather than a regulatory agreement. The agreement provides a framework for consensus building between these four countries on major issues in relation to sustainable land and water usage in the Mekong River Basin. It establishes governance arrangements including the formation of the Mekong River Commission (MRC). The MRC comprises a council, a joint committee and a secretariat. The council develops policy and the joint committee develops projects and formulates policy recommendations. A secretariat provides technical and administrative support.

The key principles underpinning the Mekong River Agreement are sustainable development and environmental protection. These are to be achieved through cooperation and a mutual benefits approach. There are only two binding clauses to the agreement. First, notification is required for intra-basin water uses and inter-basin diversions of the river and its tributaries. The second clause relates to the maintenance of minimum natural water flows. Two key projects that have developed out of the Agreement are the Water Utilisation Project (WUP) and a Basin Development Plan (BDP). The MRC also has an environment program with five key elements. These are environmental monitoring and assessment, support for appropriate responses to rapid environmental changes and emerging issues in the basin, strategic networking and coordination, capacity building and awareness raising, and research support and facilitation.

The agreement is often ignored and the commission bypassed by national governments dealing directly with each other over issues related to land and water in the Mekong River Basin. The exclusion of the MRC from such discussions undermines its ability to develop and apply consistent policies and approaches to sustainable development in the region. As part of its Environment Program, the MRC has identified the need for assessment of environmental issues which could potentially cause environmental conflict.[37] This includes recognition of the need for improved methods for the management of cross-boundary conflicts.[38]

A number of areas of potential conflict have been identified. The MRC points out that 'prevention and resolution of potential conflicts arising from the increasing pressure on the natural resources in the basin is a key task of the Mekong River Commission.[39] In 2002, the commission initiated a consultancy project to examine and report on the causes and proposed methods of prevention and resolution of conflict.[40] A main recommendation in this report was for the development of 'strong and implementable policies and rules to provide a basis for clarity and consistency in decision making and regional governance'.[41] Improving awareness of the need for intergovernmental decision making will not necessarily lead to greater cooperation between governments. Mechanisms for cooperation that extend beyond the creation of intergovernmental institutions must be developed. These would be used to help prevent many issues from becoming sources of conflict – for example, through attempts to develop policy positions and principles of common interest, and to isolate and then assess potentially divisive issues according to the terms of the agreement.

Conflict management

Three factors increase the likelihood of conflict over water use: competing demands for increasingly scarce supplies of water; the reciprocal impacts of land and water uses and inadequate governance arrangements. The construction of dams is the activity most likely to lead to conflict over water. Land uses increasingly affect water flows. In countries such as those in the Mekong River Basin, the trans-boundary nature of the impacts has the potential to increase conflict between countries. Dams often have severe human impacts and environmental impacts are well documented such as those mentioned in the earlier discussion of the Nile and Murray Darling River basins. Physical transformation of rivers; changes to flow regimes, detrimental effects on riverine and terrestrial ecosystems; downstream impacts such as reductions in silt deposition, changes to floodplains and deltas and a decline in natural resources, particularly fisheries, are examples of such environmental impacts.

China has constructed large dams, the Manwan and Dachaoshan on the mainstream of the Mekong River, alongside other dams along the lower sections of the mainstream as well as numerous small-scale projects on tributaries, and hydro projects.[42] The MRC argues that 'It is high time that a well-conceived hydro strategy be integrated into any development plans for the Mekong River Basin and that the MRC places itself as a neutral mediator in this respect'.[43] However, under the Mekong River Agreement, the MRC hydropower strategy and the environmental impact assessment (EIA) procedures are not legally enforceable, and depend on the willingness of member countries to implement them, and on international donors and financing agencies to include them in project specifications. China's unilateral action and non-membership of the MRC would appear to be potentially fertile causes of conflict with the MRC and national governments in the Lower Mekong region. China's program of dam construction will increasingly affect the flow regime in the Lower Mekong.

The limitations of the Mekong River Agreement and the independent actions of member states and dialogue partners has serious implications for potential future conflict over water resources and the impacts of dam construction. Regional governance requires the willingness of member countries to surrender some sovereignty to the MRC as an international means of gaining cooperative action, and the ability of country representatives on the MRC to act in the greater regional interest. However, national governments remain dominant and do not take a sufficiently regional perspective. The MRC promotion of private funding and ownership could itself lead to future conflict over water allocations and uses, pricing control and delivery of water and power.

Dams and hydropower

Since mid-2006, the four governments signatory to the Mekong River Agreement have granted approval to Thai, Malaysian, Russian, Chinese and Vietnamese companies to investigate hydropower dam development on the Mekong. Lao PDR and more recently Myanmar are considered to have the greatest potential for hydropower development. In Lao PDR, almost all of the electricity for both local consumption and export is generated from hydropower. Hydropower is seen as a cheap, renewable and relatively clean power source that does not cause air pollution or global warming. At the same time, it provides for irrigation of large areas of land.

Dams for irrigated agriculture and hydropower are particularly significant in the north-east of Thailand, with pressure for irrigation projects to combat the effects of drought, irregular rainfall and poor soil quality for farmers in this region. The focus of development is large-scale irrigation projects with multipurpose hydropower irrigation dams or solely irrigation dams with dam development the cause of considerable conflict.

Vietnam, located at the mouth of the Mekong River, does not want upstream developments that will increase salinity, alum and acid in water and soils, particularly in the dry season. The nature of the impacts of dam building will differ according to the location. Some impacts will be predictable, others will not. What are hardest to foresee are the cumulative effects of several dams.

Impacts of dam building on other waterways in the region provide useful insights into possible impacts of dam developments in the Mekong River Basin. The following discussion of the Yali dam and Pak Moon dam illustrate the lack of capacity to prevent or reduce impacts of dam developments.

Yali dam

Yali dam on the Sesan River in Vietnam, approximately seventy kilometres north of the Cambodian border, has caused detrimental environmental and social impacts downstream. The Yali dam was built in 1993, two years before the Mekong River Agreement, at an estimated cost of US one billion dollars. The Russian and Ukraine governments financed the dam, with technical support provided by Japan, Switzerland and Sweden.[44] Environmental impact assessment was conducted around the project site and did not include impacts on downstream countries. Downstream impacts include irregular hydrological patterns, changes to vegetation, water quality, wildlife and fisheries numbers, migratory patterns and habitats and social hardship.

Changes to the timing and intensity of floods in downstream areas have occurred, with water releases from the Yali dam believed responsible for this. These floods have included powerful surges of water resulting in the loss of lives, homes, agricultural land and livestock, with village life severely disrupted. Loss and damage to boats and fishing gear has also occurred. Irregular dry-season hydrological patterns have been observed, with lower than usual water levels. Hydrological changes are also blamed for a decline in aquatic plants used as a food sources downstream.

Water quality has changed due to increases in turbidity, blue green algae and water temperature. It has also been suggested that contaminated materials were used in the construction of the dam.[45] Local people have experienced health problems after drinking or bathing in the water.

Health problems include skin and eye infections, ear nose throat and chest complaints and gastrological upsets of nausea, stomach cramps and diarrhoea. A number of animals, including water monitor lizards, iguanas, soft-shelled turtles, several species of mammals and fish, have been affected by the unnatural water fluctuation and changes to habitats and migratory patterns. The changes to the river hydrology, ecology and biodiversity have resulted in considerable suffering and hardship for local people living along the Sesan River; they want it returned to its natural state.

Pak Moon dam

The Pak Moon dam is a hydroelectricity dam located in Thailand. It was funded by the World Bank and the government of Thailand and built by the Electricity Generating Authority of Thailand (EGAT).[46] Both the World Bank and EGAT claimed that there would not be any adverse impacts from the dam development on local villagers who relied on the river for fishing. Plans for mitigating local impacts were confined to the relocation of village people who were directly affected by the rising waters of the dam. Since dam construction, there has been a decline in the numbers of fish in the river and many families have suffered as a result. Compensation packages were negotiated with the Thai government, yet subsequent changes in leadership did not see this commitment carried out.

Local people have protested calling for the spill gates on the dam to be permanently opened.[47] A protest village was formed on the land surrounding the dam with in excess of 3,700 villagers agitating for the spill gates to be opened. This protest was organised by the Assembly of the Poor, a community activist group that represents the interests of villagers opposed to development projects. Obstacles were set up to prevent maintenance work on the generators. The government established an independent committee to assess the impacts of the dam and to make recommendations for future management. One of the recommendations of this committee was to open the spill gates for four months, but this and other recommendations were not seen as feasible by EGAT. Subsequently, the government ordered the opening of all spill gates for one year while further research was conducted to study the impacts. One research team recommended keeping the gates open for a further five years with another recommending the decommissioning of the dam. Ultimately, the government decided to keep the gates open for eight months each year. Villagers continued to demand that the spill gates remain permanently open.[48]

The examples of the Yali and the Pak Moon dams highlight the negative environmental and social impacts experienced as a result of such developments. The Pak Moon example illustrates different interests and priorities amongst key stakeholder groups, disagreement over data and structural differences resulting in power imbalances. Interest conflict has also resulted from high levels of mistrust.[49]

Both dam developments highlight a lack of coordination and divergent interests between different stakeholder groups, particularly government representatives and the people. Villagers were not involved in the planning stages and as key stakeholders did not have an opportunity to voice their concerns until after decisions had been made. Likewise, key stakeholders in neighbouring countries downstream were not included. The developments reveal problems with the collection and reliability of information on the environmental and social impacts of dam developments and the lack of adequate compensatory mechanisms for those who have been adversely affected by such developments.

Policy-making mediation is a process that can assist in future sustainable development in the Mekong River Basin. Policy-making mediation entails the recognition of rights and responsibilities, and equitable and sustainable practices in natural resource management to avoid future conflict. Prevention, management and resolution of conflict can result in improved quality of life and sustainable economic and resource development. The goal of preventative mediation in the Mekong River Basin is to uphold the main principles espoused in the Mekong River Agreement, and to keep vital eco-systems and cultures viable while engaging in sustainable economic development activities. Key issues in the application of a policy-making mediation process in the Mekong River Basin are considered below.

Stage 1: intake: determining appropriateness to mediate

Determining appropriateness to mediate involves consideration of key stakeholders who should participate in the mediation process and in what roles.

Who should participate in policy-making mediation in the Mekong River Basin and in what roles?

Key stakeholders for dam and hydropower developments include representatives of the governments and relevant line agencies of all the countries in the Mekong River Basin including Lao PDR, Cambodia, Vietnam and Thailand as well as China and Burma (Myanmar) upstream. Currently only the countries in the lower Mekong River Basin are signatories to the Mekong River Agreement. Developments taking place in the upper reaches (in China and Myanmar) need to be considered as an overall management plan for the river and its tributaries is worked out. Local community involvement is required, as well as representation of relevant non-government and environmental organisations. Other parties involved are the Mekong River Commission, donor organisations and relevant corporations and companies affected.

Stage 2: orientation

For the mediation to be effective, it is important that the process and rules be accepted as appropriate to the parties involved. These vary, according to the context and cultural rules and norms that operate in different settings.

How might the mediation rules be applied in a culturally sensitive manner with the parties in the Mekong River Basin?

Stage 3: information sharing: fact finding

A main need for all countries involved is the provision of adequate time and resources for reliable environmental, social and economic impact assessment planning and management. Environmental planning and management issues must be properly identified at the initial stages of project development inclusive of trans-boundary, national, state, regional, provincial and district level impacts. The reliability of environmental impact assessments (EIA) is often questionable due to unreliable data and inadequate time and resources being provided for a proper assessment. Trans-boundary impacts are difficult to assess and are often not even considered. In some disputes the EIA itself has been a main source of conflict, with the integrity of the current EIA questioned. This is due to the project developer often being responsible for contracting the company to conduct the EIA.

Local concerns include impacts on fisheries, destruction of crops from increased salinity in the irrigation water near dams, and outstanding claims or inadequate compensation for those villagers affected. In Lao PDR, hydropower is the major natural resource to provide electricity for manufactured exports and for socio-economic development as well as a main source of national electricity supply, especially in rural areas. Although one of the cleanest sources of energy, significant environmental and social problems have resulted from the manner and rate of dam building and hydropower in the region. Environmental concerns relate to the loss of forest cover and biodiversity. Populations most affected are often subsistence-based ethnic minorities who live in remote forest locations and who 'often have little capacity to cope with the impacts and disruptions of large infrastructure projects'.[50]

Like Lao PDR, Vietnam is also concerned about adverse impacts of resettling local ethnic minorities, loss of forest and biodiversity and aquatic ecosystems. The erosion of the riverbanks is a further concern for Vietnam due to its downstream location. Particular concerns relate to increased levels of acid and alum in water and soil caused by the discharge from upstream reservoirs as well as irrigation practices. Adequate water levels and volume are needed to clean the soil and dilute water supplies.

Dam construction for power and irrigation has been described as '...the most sensitive issue of all water-related projects in the Mekong Basin'.[51] Perceived benefits include energy, irrigation, flood control and employment but there are numerous social and environmental impacts: changes to the flow of the river and the river ecology, water quality and seismic instability, and obstruction of migratory fish and destruction of fishery habitats. Social impacts such as the relocation of people and the flooding of historical sites and forestland, and increased health problems are considerable. Downstream countries receive few benefits from hydropower developments but will be left with the environmental and social impacts.

Local Mekong River committees have limited technical and legal capacity to assume a coordinating role or to provide policy advice. Line agencies are mainly responsible for dams and hydropower and other water related projects. In spite of the existence of the Mekong River Agreement, 'there are still no appropriate mechanisms to deal with trans-boundary conflicts'.[52]

Stage 4: identification of main issues: agenda setting

Issues and priorities for each country vary according to population, level of development and situation on the Mekong River. For instance, Thailand has its water resources virtually fully developed. This is in marked contrast to Lao PDR, which has a smaller population and a less affluent economy with scarce development of water resources. Cambodia is still recovering from years of war and is more concerned with impacts from upstream countries. Likewise, Vietnam located at the mouth of the Mekong, does not want upstream developments that will increase salinity levels, particularly in the dry season.

It is the role of the mediator to identify with the parties the main mutual issues in neutral and shared language and to order these by priority. The listing is then used as the basis for future negotiations with a focus on shared issues rather than differences. Three main issues were identified:

1. Land use
   land tenure/ ownership/migration
   land conservation – protected areas
   irrigated agriculture
2. Resources
   fisheries
   forestry
3. Water
   dams / hydropower
   navigation
   flooding.

Stage 5: developing options: mapping the conflict

Choose an issue identified in stage 4 and map the interests, needs and concerns of main parties. Remember location on the river as well as level of development and resources.

Conflict Map

Who?
Needs:
Concerns:
Fears:

Who?   Who?
Needs: Needs:
Concerns: Issue   Concerns:
Fears: Fears:

                Who?
                Needs:
                Concerns
                Fears:

Brainstorm to generate as many solutions as possible.

Stage 6: selecting options: negotiation and decision making

The mutual gains approach to negotiation is particularly useful in complex environments involving multiple parties (see chapter 4). It is consistent with the role of the Mekong River Commission to coordinate and promote sustainable development and management of water and land resources for the mutual benefit of the countries and people living in the Mekong River Basin.

1. *How might a mutual gains approach be applied in the Mekong River Basin? (Refer chapter 2 for details of the four stages in the mutual gains approach of preparation, value creation, value distribution and follow-through.)*

2. *In the preparation stage, consider the best alternative to a negotiated agreement (BATNA) and the worst alternative to a negotiated agreement (WATNA) for each party.*

3. *Bring order to the range of options generated in the designing options stage and make links between similar or complementary options. Evaluate the appropriateness and feasibility of particular options.*

Stage 7: agreement preparation and implementation

A main feature of policy-making mediation is development of an enforceable agreement.

Draft an agreement for the issue you have identified and mapped. Include an implementation plan.

Conclusion

Conflict prevention and management in the Mekong River Basin is a continuous process that needs to be rediscovered and reapplied to new or reorganised sets of social, environmental and economic relationships. It is essential that the interplay between the environment and development is recognised and incorporated as a central feature of policy development in the Mekong River Basin and that the relationships between natural resources and human interaction, including physical, emotional, social, cultural and spiritual aspects are recognised. The aim of policy-making mediation in the Mekong River Basin is to facilitate a process whereby the main principles espoused in the Mekong River Agreement can be implemented. This approach can assist in anticipating complex and difficult issues and the planning of processes to deal with them. Policy-making mediation is a process that allows for consensus building in the spirit of the Mekong River Agreement but also allows for the development of polices and legally binding processes to enact effective regional governance. It is useful for the development and implementation of standards and procedures in rules and regulations for water, land and natural resource use in the Mekong River Basin. The effective management and prevention of conflict, reflected in legislation, agreements and policy frameworks and procedures, can help protect this, and other regions of the world, for current and future generations.

9

International peace and security

Building and maintaining international peace and security requires consideration of the processes of economic and social development, international regime building and support for democracy. An emphasis is on conciliatory approaches and the application of non-violent means of conflict management with much less emphasis on coercive strategies. The focus is on preventive strategies – the earlier the better; the re-conceptualisation of different crises and alternative ways of dealing with them. In international peace making, there is a synergy between economic development, representative governance, promotion of human rights, protection of individual and collective identities and the achievement of stable peaceful relations between peoples.

Lack of acceptance of negotiated solutions and willingness to contemplate violence are most likely where there is economic underdevelopment, authoritarian rule and a generalised culture of violence supporting the use of weapons as a means of settling disputes. The combination is likely to result in gross violations of human rights, or genocide. Conflicts are likely to result in a breakdown of civil law and order and open warfare among armed groups in situations wherever there is little political legitimacy, or sectarian or communal politics are dominant, and factional groups adopt armed strategies and repressive regimes impose violent responses.

Intervention based on faulty or wrong analysis is likely to exacerbate rather than alleviate the presenting as well as the underlying problems. Most violent conflicts stem from highly unequal power relationships.

The conflicts are concerned with the dynamics of power, empowerment of the disempowered, mobilisation of resources, confrontation and management or resolution of current and subsequent conflict.

Three general techniques for the prevention of violence are

- avoiding conflicts through the adequate supplies of valued goods, minimising demands, or developing super-ordinate goals
- preventing disruptive conflict from crossing the violence threshold through techniques of suppression and regulation
- resolving the conflict through mediation, conciliation, negotiation or other conciliatory techniques.[1]

The greater the level of violence, the more difficult it is to settle conflicts peaceably. The challenge for the future is one based on early intervention moving from systems based on coercion and threats to ones based on trust and cooperation. This chapter discusses global conflicts in terms of sources of conflict and actors, conflict analysis, prevention, containment, transformation and reconciliation. The use of private military forces is considered as well as the use of technology.

Sources of conflict and actors

As mentioned earlier in this text, conflict generally arises from competitions for scarce resources. This may be a small localised conflict or an interstate or intra-state conflict. The term interstate in the international conflict literature is used to describe a conflict that is occurring within a nation state whereas an intra-state conflict is conflict with other nation states. Conflict at an international level is generally over scarce resources such as land and territory and natural resources including oil and water. Conflict may arise from a change in availability of the resource and/or a change in how it is accessed or distributed. For instance, many disputes over fertile land for agriculture and water arise from climate change and government access and distribution policies and practices. Conflict may arise from differing ideological beliefs, values and practices that lead to the development of different group identities, cultures and practices. Conflict is more likely to arise in circumstances where there are marked class differences in terms of poverty and wealth and associated economic, social and political opportunities that are afforded to some but denied to others. Economic conflict is on the rise in western neo-liberal societies where we have witnessed the growth in numbers of those with extreme wealth and those who live in poverty, with young people over-represented in this latter group.

International disputes are often referred to as 'old wars' and 'new wars'.[2] Old wars are generally between sovereign states whereas new wars are often both interstate and intra-state. Old wars are generally before World War II and predominantly involved aggressions on the territory of another state and the defence of this state and territory. In more recent years, and particularly since 9/11 and increased terrorism and use of technology in warfare, we are witnessing a second wave of new wars that are quite different to those post World War II. Old war conflicts involved armed forces with most casualties being soldiers. Battles were clearly defined and orchestrated with clarity on who the enemy and allies were. Armed forces were fighting for their country, nationalism and freedom. Since World War II we have seen a relative hiatus with the Cold War (1947–1991). Following the Cold War, we have seen the dominance of Western liberal democracies as the preferred form of government and humanitarian intervention. Non-democratic states have questioned the impartiality of the United Nations when imposing Western democratic models of government under the guise of peace building.

We have also seen the emergence of new types of conflicts where the enemy is not so easily identifiable such as in Vietnam and Iraq, with soldiers finding it difficult to distinguish between combatants and civilians. There may be a variety of different actors involved in armed conflicts including warlords, militia forces and rebels. The important role of women, children and members of minority groups as key actors is often overlooked. Each party may have different resource needs and means available to them. Scarce resources may be tangible such as land, money and technology or intangible such as values, recognition and possibly retribution. Accordingly, these intangible resources encompass notions of justice, human rights and morality. International interests may be more evident with other states, or bodies – legal or illegal, financing or backing different groups in the conflict in pursuit for their own interests. For example, the involvement of the British in the Gulf War was primarily related to protecting oil resources for the British.

New conflicts are more likely to extend to ideological beliefs with specific battles and victories not always easily identified or understood and often with far greater violence inflicted upon local communities. The war on terror is an example of this, with it being difficult to know who the enemy is and when and where it might strike. This fear is met with increased sanctions and regulation by governments on their own citizens in the name of national security and public safety. Isis has provided governments with opportunities to increase control and surveillance of their own citizens. In doing so, they are treating their own citizens as possible enemies as opposed to targeted activities towards an external enemy during old wars.

Interestingly, since the start of Covid-19, Isis has received little mention as the government shifted focus to the enactment of laws to control citizen movement with the imposition of curfews, time limits on outdoor activity, travel restrictions and peaceful assembly unlawful, in response to the threat of health security. A number of minority protest groups are banding together in the name of civil liberties under the banner of a particular issue such as 'anti-vaccination' or 'anti 5G' and 'anti-racism'. At the heart of these protests is a call for freedom and the protection of civil liberties. The use of oppressive tactics to prevent peaceful protests is an attack on freedom and autonomy.[3] The restoration of freedom and autonomy through democratic processes is a focus of international conflict resolution. A British judge is reputed to have once said that everything in England is permitted unless specifically prohibited by law. That saying is apt for a free and democratic society like Australia. United Nations conventions include safeguards for freedom of movement and association.

In terms of conflict management, this situation highlights the significance of an understanding of human needs and human rights and the importance of good governance. This includes considering the appropriateness of the key parties involved in decision-making, the narrative, the timeliness and credibility of those delivering the message and the timeliness, appropriateness and feasibility of the action plan. Caution and vigilance is required to ensure that after Covid-19 human rights are restored and that this is not seen as an opportunity to use these human rights restrictions in the longer term for other purposes.

An example of this is the increase in police discretionary powers in some states and territories in Australia in response to the problem of alcohol-related violence in public entertainment areas. Increased police discretionary powers granted included fines, bans, exclusions, and move-on powers. These discretionary powers have general application and are not confined to the problem that led to their enactment.[4] This has led to claims of discrimination and the targeting of young people, and Indigenous youth in particular, for unnecessary police initiated contact and intervention. This includes reports of indirect and direct racism by some police. Direct racism includes overt acts such as verbal and physical abuse with indirect racism more subtle, often not named, and frequently denied by the perpetrator. The stopping of Indigenous young people for random police checks moreso than non-Indigenous youth is an example of indirect racism.[5] These powers mean that young people can be moved on from public places and recreation areas such as parks and shopping centres at the discretion of the police and many live in fear of the police pulling them over at any time for no particular reason. This results in increased fear from the young person and their family members, with decreased confidence that the police will assist if they are a victim of crime.

Conflict analysis

International conflict analysis requires close attention to the identification of the early stages and escalation of conflict so as to able to respond early on to prevent further escalation or to engage in de-escalation. Each conflict is unique and often unpredictable in terms of speed of escalation and time required for de-escalation.[6] Careful scoping of the stage of the conflict is required to determine the most appropriate conflict prevention or management approach at a specific point in time. Conflict scoping requires gaining an understanding of the issues underlying the conflict and the significance of these to different individuals and groups. These sources of conflict will be relational, contextual and internal. This includes differences within and between groups that may hinder conflict resolution processes. For instance, a person purporting to represent a key stakeholder group may only have the support of a minority of group members or possibly none at all. Often what is seen publicly and reported in the media, is at the micro level and likely to be sensationalised such as a violent altercation between disputing factions at a protest rally. Attention is required to assess the macro factors including social structures and institutions to fully understand the social and political context and interplay between observed micro aggressions and the not so visible social and political institutions. This includes an analysis of the power of key constituents including power over economic resources, power to inflict harm, and power to promote healing.[7] This also includes the identification of key 'third parties', often neighbouring states, and analysis of their political and military influence on resolving and fuelling the conflict.[8]

International conflict analysis shows repeated instances where tensions were evident and widely known at both state and intra-state levels yet there has been a reluctance to get involved in many disputes, that do not involve a national interest, by members of the international community. Protracted social conflicts often have interstate and intra-state aspects to them and are often characterised by long and violent conflict over basic human needs. Game theory (see chapter 4) is used widely in conflict management in situations of war and entrenched violence. More recent developments have focused on the need to fully understand relationships to prevent conflict; the prevention of war requires an understanding of interstate and intra-state relationships. An increased emphasis is on problem-solving (see chapter 6) with the clear identification of main issues in dispute, needs, concerns and fears, best and worst alternatives to a negotiated agreement, future planning and feasibility testing.

Main international conflict management activities are conflict prevention, conflict containment, conflict transformation and justice and reconciliation. These are cyclical and overlapping processes with conflict prevention a key aspect of reconciliation. Ideally, most effort is put into conflict prevention early on in a conflict. However, it is more likely that the first point of intervention is conflict containment.

Figure 7.1

International conflict management cycle

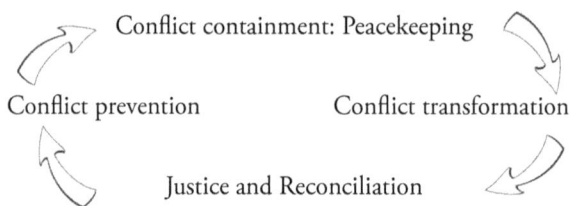

Conflict containment: Peacekeeping

Conflict prevention   Conflict transformation

Justice and Reconciliation

Conflict prevention

The aim of conflict prevention is to develop and support conditions that are conducive to peace and that negate the development of armed conflict. Early prevention involves the identification of early warning signs of tense relationships with late prevention aimed at the possibility of violence.[9] Prevention involves fact finding to clearly identify the level of conflict and main issues in dispute with diplomacy and mediation used to address these. This includes assessment of the influence of structural factors related to geography and natural resources, distribution of economic wealth and resources, gender, ethnic and cultural diversity and representation by minority interest groups. Key considerations are timing and 'readiness' for conflict resolution.

This includes developing confidence in the conflict prevention process and the mediators, the design, application and adequate resourcing of conflict prevention activities, which may include the deployment of armed troops and personnel to enforce the peace agreement, and possibly the development of peace zones. A key international actor in conflict prevention is the United Nations, including the General Assembly and Security Council, diplomats, peacebuilding commissions and missions. Other key actors represent different segments of government and society at local, state and intra-state levels and might include the military, non-government organisations and private corporations. Neighbouring states and international states with a vested interest in the region are influential in terms of escalation or de-escalation of the conflict. They may be involved in the supply of arms or other efforts that support continued violence.[10]

The aim of intervention by a third-party mediator is to diffuse the conflict by creating a forum that promotes a fair and open process for discussion, reconciliation and future planning while endeavouring to redress power imbalances. This includes moving beyond rhetoric to gain a genuine understanding of the issues in dispute and recognising the nature of the dispute in terms of interstate and intra-state aspects and when it is and is not appropriate for an external third party to intervene in a national conflict. In situations where mediation does not result in a resolution, an adjudication process might be adopted with a decision made in accordance with international law by the Permanent Court of Arbitration at The Hague in The Netherlands.

Conflict containment: peacekeeping

In international contexts, conflict containment involves international peacekeeping and humanitarian intervention by the United Nations and international organisations aimed at protection. Peacekeeping gained prominence in 1956 when the United Nations intervened in the Suez crisis. Peacemaking interventions involve the use of 'impartial' international military forces to contain conflict through (1) monitoring and (2) enforcement interventions. These military forces might be interstate or extra-state and may be external to the UN. International organisations that play a key role in peacekeeping are the North Atlantic Treaty Organisation (NATO) from 1994 and the European Union (EU) since 2003.

Monitoring interventions are focused on observations with enforcement interventions including non-violent interventions and coercive tactics. Force is condoned in self-defence and if deemed necessary as an intervention of last resort - that is proportional to the problem encountered. Peacekeeping interventions are more likely to succeed if they are safe against attack, clearly separate the warring parties and detect and prevent cease fire violations.[11]

International intervention in the affairs of a sovereign state is counter to Article 2(7) of the United Nations Charter that is designed to protect sovereign states from outside interference and acts of aggression by other states. However, international intervention is supported in United Nations human rights declarations and conventions post World War II in the Cold War period (1944–1962) and include the Universal Declaration of Human Rights 1948 and the Genocide Convention 1948. During and beyond this Cold War period until the 1990s, the United Nations Security Council, comprising the United States, the United Kingdom, China, Russia and France, did not approve UN humanitarian intervention in sovereign states. The 1990s have witnessed humanitarian interventions by the United Nations in Iraq (1991), Somalia (1992), Rwanda (1994) and by the North Atlantic Treaty Organisation (NATO) in Kosovo. Questions arise as to the motivation to intervene and state interests.

Reasons for non-intervention include states having the right at law to manage their own internal affairs, concerns that humanitarian intervention using force can inflict further violence and abuse, humanitarian intervention may be a guise for states to intervene to pursue their own national interests, or that there is no national interest to warrant involvement. This last scenario of no state interest is the most likely reason for non-intervention in the genocide of the Tutsi in Rwanda (7 April 1994–15 July 1994) and the Rohingas in Myanmar (August 2017–).

This raises moral questions of when states should intervene in the affairs of other states, for what purpose and in what manner.

In 2005, the United Nations General Assembly adopted Responsibility to Protect (R2P) principles for the protection of people in danger that was affirmed by the United Nations Security Council. This is underpinned by three pillars: (1) a state is responsible for protecting its people from crimes against humanity, war crimes and genocide; (2) the international community is responsible for assisting a state to protect its people; and (3) the international community will use peaceful processes with force condoned if a state is inflicting harm on its citizens.[12] If it is considered to be state inflicted violence, the UN Security Council will consider an international response. This clearly places responsibility upon the state to protect its people while providing for armed intervention by the international community. There has been inconsistent application of R2P and criticisms of imperialism with the domination of stronger states over weaker ones.

Conflict transformation

Conflict transformation moves beyond de-escalation, prevention and containment. Conflict transformation is concerned with changes to political, economic and social structures and relationships. This includes effective future management of the issues in conflict and recognition that conflict is organic. Transformation requires ongoing conflict management strategies rather than a static view of conflict that cessation of violence is resolution of the conflict.

As mentioned in the opening chapter, conflict is a normal part of everyday life and – regardless of the size, complexity and level of the conflict – requires ongoing management and strategic intervention if the conflicting parties are in continuing interaction into the future. In international disputes, this may require legislative and policy change as well as local, bilateral and multilateral agreements, particularly with neighbouring states. As discussed in the previous chapter, policy-making mediation is particularly well suited to international conflicts as political, economic and social change requires culturally appropriate institutions and processes to support this. An effective mediation process would see positive changes occurring throughout the earlier process of prevention and containment that then develop further into transformation. This is a higher order outcome that moves beyond problem-solving and the stopping of atrocities to the application of principles of natural and social justice that embody respect, dignity and rights and responsibilities. In the long-term transformation requires an analysis of emotions, perceptions and spiritual aspects that influence motivation, quality of relationships and well-being.[13]

The identification of issues that have led to the alienation of different groups will assist in building trust and a greater understanding and ability to move forward by not repeating past mistakes and maintaining social order through cohesion rather than control. Positive reframing by the mediator of negative perceptions to positive attitudes will assist in relationship building and the prevention of a return to hostilities. New issues, goals and tactics will emerge as each party endeavours to find the most successful outcome. The aim of the mediator is to develop mutual goals that meet the needs, concerns, interests and fears of factional groups to develop collaborative processes into the future. More powerful groups will require convincing that co-operation is in their best interests. This requires skilful mediator intervention for inclusive processes that address minority group concerns and political, economic and social inclusion. At the heart of this is sharing power and redressing structural inequality. This is not easily achieved, particularly in disputes where one party has been granted the disputed territory or resources, as in the case of Israel and Palestine. In territorial disputes that involve UN intervention, priority is generally given to the state that occupied the territory before the conflict. Longstanding conflicts however may have seen numerous territorial changes before the current conflict.

The transformation of relationships requires adequate resourcing of rebuilding processes to address the issues of the conflicting parties. If basic needs are not met, it is not likely that relationships will be transformed.

For some states, this requires mobilisation of resources from the international community. New relationships, perceptions and understandings and social structures are required. Peace and stability are achieved by acknowledging the interdependence of the need for the development of new ways of being that are non-violent and that promote community and social cohesion. Women's organisations, and self-help and mutual support groups contribute to the well-being of communities.[14]

Justice and reconciliation

A key focus of reconciliation of conflict is the achievement and maintenance of harmony in the long-term. This includes positive non-violent change in personal, group and state relationships and behaviours. This is a long-term goal aimed at embedding goodwill and collaborative processes to sustain trusting relationships in the long term. Reconciliation involves a deeper level of political, structural, cultural and relational change established during conflict transformation. Peacebuilding and stability in the longer term requires the restoration of a functioning government, security forces and essential services. Reconciliation aims to prevent violence through new ways of living and working collaboratively to reinforce justice and new ways of being into the future that promote harmony and avoid history repeating itself.

A focus on justice and reconciliation arose following World War II with the establishment of international courts and tribunals and Truth Commissions. The main court used by the UN is the International Court of Justice that deals with interstate conflicts. A further court is the International Criminal Court that can investigate war crimes and crimes against humanity including genocide. Truth Commissions are bodies established to investigate human rights abuses that have occurred during a particular conflict. The commissioners engage in a process of collecting information on abuse that provides an opportunity for victims of abuse to tell their stories and to be heard by perpetrators. They then decide on who is responsible and what an appropriate response is. These responses are underpinned by principles of restorative justice discussed in chapter 7. Possible responses are full amnesty, partial amnesty, restoration for victims that may include compensation and an apology. At times, difficulties have arisen in identifying perpetrators and victims with some people considered to be both victims and perpetrators. A key question is, who benefitted from the injustice and what role did they play? Decisions need to be made on what rights to focus on, with gender-based violence often excluded. In some instances such as in the genocide in Rwanda in 1994, Truth Commission decisions were inconsistent, victims were not compensated and some perpetrators were not held to account. This raises questions about the appropriateness of this process to make determinations on crimes of such magnitude, resourcing issues, and expertise and impartiality of the commissioners.

In the early 1990s, the concept of peacekeeping was expanded to support political, security, economic and humanitarian needs. Activities undertaken by the UN to restore sustainable peace into the future in response to 'new wars' are focused on the disarming of parties, the restoration of order, the repatriation of refugees, the monitoring of elections, the rebuilding of institutions, community inclusion and community development.[15] Subsequent UN peace operations were heavily criticised for failure in the delivery of sustainable peacemaking efforts. In early 2000, the Brahimi Report made recommendations to the UN Secretary-General to improve peacekeeping operations. The report noted that the UN needed to carefully consider the appropriateness of a peacekeeping response following consideration of the unique features of a conflict. The report provided increased clarity on appropriate responsibilities, roles and tasks of the UN to identify and defeat ongoing post-conflict violence and aggression. Many of these recommendations were adopted by the UN resulting in improved outcomes.[16] In 2015, the High Level Independent Panel on United Nations Peace Operations (HIPPO) presented a report to the UN Secretary-General in response to concerns that the UN was not well prepared to respond to changes in local and regional conflicts that now had an overlay of extremism and terrorism. The report recommended new approaches into the future including an increased focus on (1) conflict prevention using mediation, (2) the core responsibility of protection of civilians, (3) greater clarity on the use of force in peacekeeping, (4) political vigilance to support reconciliation and (5) addressing the underlying issues in dispute.[17]

Private military forces

An added complexity is the increased use of mercenaries and private military forces employed by governments, warlords, private individuals, companies or organisations. These mercenaries are paid to deliver prescribed services to their employer that may involve provision of weapons, military transport, technology that might include drones or intelligence, troops, and other supplies and services. These mercenaries are often ex-military elite personnel from forces around the world who work as private contractors or run private military companies for hire. These private military forces may consistitute a significant military force and operation and might also be employed by states as private contractors to deliver humanitarian aid and peacekeeping activities. These private armed forces are not publically state or UN sanctioned. This raises considerable legal, ethical and moral issues. In a neo liberal capitalist world of privatised services we must now acknowledge that we have private armies that may or may not have state affiliations who are in effect guns for hire with the main aim of financial profit. Under Chapter VII of the UN Charter, Article 41, the UN Security Council has the authority to apply sanctions that support conflict prevention, peacekeeping, transformation, justice and reconciliation. The aim of these sanctions is to support the establishment of peaceful processes, prevent non-constitutional activity, protect human rights and constrain terrorism. These sanctions might include arms embargos and restrictions on commodities, travel, assets and finances.

Technology, artificial intelligence and peacemaking

As mentioned in chapter 3, with the advancement of technology alongside artificial intelligence, we are faced with new challenges in content consumption which can extend to gradual psychological manipulation. Often in peacekeeping the focus is on how technology can be used as a tool for communication, strategy, surveillance and to aid military operations. However, it is crucial to consider how artificial intelligence is now being used to manipulate people into thinking and behaving in particular ways. This includes the encouragement of polarised political views and oppositional behaviours through the use of cognitive behavioural techniques that promote addictive behaviours. This manipulation is done by persistent vested interest advertising sending targeted and biased information, which may result in influencing individuals gradually to think in a different way or be aligned with the ideas presented in the content curated specifically for them. This manipulation can be seen in outcomes of varying scale, for example influencing the purchase of a retail item or in more dangerous circumstances influencing political election results and extremist rallying.

This manipulation activity is driven by capitalist ideology that is ultimately aimed at profit. As is often the case in democratic capitalist societies, industries are left to self-regulate. This is extremely problematic when the main motivation is profit. Ultimately, this manipulation is eroding the core values of democratic societies and is leading to an increase in violence between diverse groups whose views are formed on the basis of targeted misinformation and disinformation inciting violence being sent to particular individual and groups. We are all vulnerable to this manipulation and most of us are addicted to our smartphones. However, artificial intelligence is being used to identify and target vulnerabilities and those who may be more likely to change their opinion, or be influenced by friends or what they see on social media. This can create a false sense of human connection and sense of purpose for those who are lonely and socially disconnected. Those with pre-existing mental health or cognitive disorders that include distortions of reality are particularly vulnerable, as they are also prone to social isolation.

The focus of the United Nations is on keeping up with technological change but not necessarily critiquing the value of these new technologies from a philosophical and ethical standpoint. The United Nations Commission on Science and Technology for Development (CSTD) is a subsidiary body of the United Nations Economic and Social Council (ECOSOC). It commenced in 1992 as a forum for states, non-government organisations, academics, business, and civil society to provide expert advice to the UN on future directions in policy development. The aim is to identify and respond globally to challenges and opportunities for science and technology to support common policies for sustainable development to achieve the UN Sustainable Development Goals. This includes consideration of contribution to humanity, governance and frontier technology development. This has included the internet of things (IoT), big data analytics, artificial intelligence, and bio-tech and gene editing. A focus is on developing countries to ensure states and populations are not left behind in times of rapid technological change.

A main argument in the 2015 report of the United Nations expert panel on technology and innovation in peacekeeping was that UN peacekeeping missions in contemporary complex environments can only succeed with the effective use of the latest technologies. It was recommended that a 'tech map' and an 'information map' be developed for each mission.[18] The tech map would identify needs and capabilities for informed decision-making with the information map providing clarity for headquarters and missions on information collection, storage, use, sharing and authorisation. It was suggested that UN peacekeeping activities have been hampered by limitations to available technology. In some instances, state military and police have had access to far more sophisticated technology than UN peacekeepers and some states with more advanced technologies are not wanting to be involved in UN peacekeeping operations because of this. Priorities identified by the expert panel with implementation guidelines included: mandated applications of technology to protect civilians, assist operations and communications between mission networks, information sharing platforms, security and safety, and medical support. They refer to 'digital peacekeepers', who include military, police and civilians equipped with the latest technologies. Ongoing training is essential to ensure that they are up to date and competent in the application of new and emerging technologies with adequate resourcing to do so.

Conclusion

This discussion of international conflict, peace and security highlights the importance of conflict prevention through timely localised responses to bring about positive change, with coercive intervention by foreigners a last resort. Nation building requires legislation, policy, treaties and conventions that support gender and racial equality, social inclusion of minority groups, appropriate and affordable accommodation, access to quality healthcare, education, training and employment opportunities and a safety net for those unable to provide for themselves and their families. These are the hallmarks of a civilised society and it is in times of peace that foreign intervention is most appropriate in terms of assisting less developed states with nation building. Wealthier states in the international community can no longer be passive bystanders witnessing other states living in poverty often following natural disasters that are on the rise. Humanity calls for increased humanitarian interventions that assist with local community development and rebuilding including opportunities for education and trade that are not reliant upon profiteering by wealthy countries or multinational companies. It requires careful consideration of the appropriateness and regulation of private military forces and the use of artificial intelligence.

In terms of external foreign intervention to stop conflict, questions remain about the appropriateness of the imposition of neo-liberal views and responsiveness to cultural issues when forming new political structures. Ongoing consideration of power and resource differentials is required as mostly it is more wealthy states intervening in the affairs of less economically developed states. The level of support from the international community and possible hidden national interests and agendas, requires careful scrutiny. The complexity of so many actors and the size of the task – especially when a new state is formed or there is a change in regime, raises issues of cost and long-term support and sustainability into the future. We look forward to a world where all people are treated with dignity and respect. As members of the international community, we are asked to engage in inclusive and conciliatory processes that build community and provide a good life for all as part of a global movement for a sustainable future. This begins at home and questions as a starting point the true quality of our relationships and interactions with others.

References

Access to Justice Advisory Committee Report (1995) Access to Justice: An Action Plan, 71.1.

Accreditation Sub-Committee (2005) National Mediation Conference http://www.mediationconference.com.au/html/implementation.html, accessed 3rd of November 2005.

Adams, R., Dominelli, L. & Payne, M. (2009) *Social Work: Themes, Issues and Critical Debates*, 3rd ed., Palgrave, London.

Adler, P. (1998) Mediation and Conflict Resolution Workshop, Latrobe University, Bundoora.

Akers, R. (2017) *Social Learning and Social Structures: A General Theory of Crime and Deviance*, Routledge, New York.

Allan, J. (2009) 'Practising Critical Social Work' in J. Allan, B. Pease & L. Briskman, *Critical Social Work*, Allen & Unwin, Melbourne.

Anonymous (2014) The Thirty-Six Strategems, http://www.cob.sjsu.edu/jiang_w/winter2012/ClassMaterials/36stratagems.pdf accessed 10 January 2014.

Arbel, R., Rodriguez, A. & Margolin, G. (2016) 'Cortisol Reactions During Family Conflict Discussions: Influences of Wives' and Husbands' Exposure to Family-of-Origin Aggression', *Psychology of Violence*, 6 (4) : 519–528.

Aloia, L. & Solomon, D. (2015) 'Conflict Intensity, Family History, and Physiological Stress Reactions to Conflict Within Romantic Relationships', *Human Communication Research*, 41: 367–389.

Astor, H. (2000) 'Rethinking Neutrality: A Theory to Inform Practice – Part 1', *Australasian Dispute Resolution Journal*, 11: 73–83.

— (2010) 'Genuine Effort in Family Dispute Resolution', *Family Matters*, 84, 61–63.

Astor, H. & Chinkin, C. (2002) *Dispute Resolution in Australia*, 2nd ed., Butterworths, NSW.

Australian Attorney-General's Department (2009) Family Violence Prevention Legal Services, Family Violence Prevention Legal Services Section, Canberra.

Australian Institute of Arbitrators and Mediators (2014) What is Mediation? http://www.iama.org.au/what-we-do/mediation accessed 30 January 2014.

Bagshaw, D. (1995) 'Mediating Family Disputes in Statutory Settings', *Australian Social Work*, 48 (4).

— (2013) 'Domestic Violence: Feminist Perspective', in D.J. Christie, ed., *Encyclopedia of Peace Psychology*, Wiley-Blackwell, New Jersey.

Bagshaw, D. & Porter, E., eds (2009) *Mediation in the Asia-Pacific: Transforming Conflicts and Building Peace*, Routledge, New York.

Bagshaw, D., Wendt, S., Zannettino, L. & Adams, V. (2013). 'Financial Abuse of Older People by Family Members: The Views and Experiences of Older Australians and Their Family Members', *Australian Social Work*, 66 (1): 86–103.

Bailey, A. & Bickerdyke, E. (2005) *Family Violence and Family Mediation*, Domestic Violence Resource Centre, Melbourne.

Beder, S. (1993) T*he Nature of Sustainable Development*, Newham, Scribe Publications, Australia.

Bell, M. (2009) *An Invitation to Environmental Sociology*, 3rd ed., Sage Publications, Newbury Park, CA.

Bilderbeek, S. ed. (1992) *Biodiversity and International Law*, Netherlands National Committee for the International Union for Conservation of Nature and Natural Resources, IOS Press, Amsterdam.

Blackburn J. & Bruce, W., eds (1995) *Mediating Environmental Conflicts: Theory and Practice*, Quorum Books, London.

Blomquist, W., Haisman, B., Dinar, A. & Bhat, A. (2005) Institutional and Policy Analysis of River Basin Management: The Murray Darling River Basin, Australia, World Bank Policy Research Working Paper 3527, World Bank, Washington.

Bloomer, L., Nelson, C., Denniff, M., Christofidou, P., Debiec, R., Thompson, J., Zukowska-Szczechowska, E., Samani, N., Charchar, F. and Thomaszewski, M. (2014). 'Coronary Artery Disease Predisposing Haplogroup 1of the Y Chromosone, Aggression and Sex Steroids – Genetic Association Analysis', *Artherosclerosis*, 233 : 160-4.

Bogo, M. (2010) *Achieving Competence in Social Work Education Through Field Education*, University of Toronto Press, Canada.

Bogo M. & Vayda E., (1987) *The Practice of Field Instruction in Social Work*, University of Toronto Press, Toronto.

Boulding, K. (1999) *Three Faces of Power*, Sage Publications Ltd., London.

Boulle, L. (2011) *Mediation, Principles, Process, Practice*, 3rd ed. Butterworths, Sydney, Australia.

Boulle, L. & Alexander, N. (2012) *Mediation – Skills and Techniques*, 2nd ed. Butterworths, Sydney.

Boulle L. & Nesci, M., (2001) *Mediation: Principles, Process, Practice*, Butterworths, Australia.

Boutros Ghali, B. (1992) An Agenda for Peace, Preventive Diplomacy, Peacemaking and Peacekeeping: Report of the Secretary-General Pursuant to the Statement Adopted by the Summit Meeting of the Security Council on 31 January 1992, United Nations, New York.

Braithwaite, J. & Strang. H. (2016) 'Connecting Philosophy and Practice', Capter 12 in J. Braithwaite & H. Strang eds. *Restorative Justice*, Routledge, New York.

Brill, N. (1995) *Working with People*, 5th ed., Longman, USA.

Burke, B. & Harrison, P. (1998) 'Anti-Oppressive Practice', in B. Burke & P. Harrison, eds, *Social Work: Themes, Issues and Critical Debates*, Macmillan, London, 229–239.

Burgess, G. & Burgess, H. (1995) 'Beyond the Limits: Dispute Resolution of Intractable Environmental Conflicts', in J. Blackburn & W. Bruce (1995).

Burraston, B., McCutcheon, J. & Watts, S. (2018) 'Relative and Absolute Deprivation's Relationship with Crime in the United States: Testing an Interaction Effect Between Income Inequality and Disadvantage', *Crime and Delinquency*, 64 (4): 542–560.

Bush R.B. (2004) 'One Size Does Not Fit All: A Pluralistic Approach to Mediator Performance Testing and Quality Assurance', *Ohio State Journal on Dispute Resolution*, 19: 965–1004.

Bush, R.B. & Folger, J. (2005) *The Promise of Mediation: Responding to Conflict Through Empowerment and Recognition*, 2nd ed., Jossey-Bass, San Francisco.

Buxton, M., Kelly, M. & Martin, J. (2003) *Environmental Conflicts in the Mekong River Basin*, School of Social Science and Planning RMIT, Melbourne.

Caflisch, L. (1998) 'Regulation of the Uses of International Watercourses', in M. Salmon, & L. de Chazornes, eds, International Watercourses: Enhancing Cooperation and Managing Conflict, World Bank Technical Paper No. 414, Washington.

Caruthers S. (1997) 'Mediation in Child Protection and the Nova Scotia Experience', *Family and Conciliation Courts Review*, 35 (1): 102–126.

Charlesworth, S. & Haynes, J. (1996) *The Fundamentals of Mediation*, The Federation Press, NSW.

Chetkow-Yanoov, B. (1991) 'Teaching Conflict Resolution at Schools of Social Work: A Proposal', *International Social Work*, 34: 57–68.

Choi, J. & Dulisse, B. (2020) 'The Importation of 'Violent' Codes of South Korean Inmates', *The Prison Journal*, 100 (3): 287-311.

Christie, N. (1977) 'Conflicts as Property', *The British Journal of Criminology*, 17 (1): 1–15.

Clements, K. & Ward, R. (1994) *Building International Community: Co-operating for Peace*, Allen & Unwin, Sydney.

Cloke, K. & Goldsmith, J. (2000) *Resolving Conflicts at Work*, Jossey Bass, San Francisco, CA.

Cobb, S. (1993) 'Empowerment and Mediation: A Narrative Perspective', *Negotiation Journal*, 9: 245–259.

Cobb, S. & Rifkin, J. (1991) 'Neutrality as a Discursive Practice: The Construction and Transformation of Narratives in Community Mediation', *Studies in Law, Politics and Society*, 11: 69–91.

Coltri, L. (2004) *Conflict Diagnosis and Alternative Dispute Resolution*, Pearson Education Inc., New Jersey.

Community Services and Health Industry Skills Council Family Counselling, Family Dispute Resolution & Children's Contact Services Project: Draft 2 Qualifications, http://www.cshisc.com.au/load_page.asp?ID=75#papers accessed 7 July 2006.

Condliffe, P. (2004) 'Arbitration: The Forgotten ADR', *Law Institute Journal*, August, Law Institute of Victoria, Melbourne, 42–46.

Conflict Resolution Network (1993) *Conflict Resolution Trainer's Manual*, Chatswood, NSW.

Cunneen, C., Goldson, B. & Russell, S. (2016) 'Juvenile Justice, Young People and Human Rights in Australia', *Current Issues in Criminal Justice*, 28 (2): 173–189.

Dalrymple, J. & Burke, B. (2006) *Anti-Oppressive Practice: Social Care and the Law*, 2nd ed., Open University Press, USA.

Dawoud, J. (2001) *Taming the Nile's Serpents: Conflict Over Water Supply*, UNESCO, New York.

De Beer, F. & Marais, M. (2005)

'Rural communities, the natural environment and development- some challenges, some successes', *Community Development Journal*, 40 (1): 50–61.

Della Noce, D.J. (2014) Mediation Policy: Theory Matters, http://mediate.com accessed 10 January.

Della Noce, D., Bush, R.B. & Folger, J. (2002) 'Clarifying the Theoretical Underpinnings of Mediation: Implications for Practice and Policy', *Pepperdine Dispute Resolution Law Journal*, 3: 38–65.

Deutsch, M. & Coleman, P., eds, (2000) *The Handbook of Conflict Resolution*, Jossey-Bass, San Francisco.

DeVito J. (1997) *Human Communication*, Addison Wesley, New York.

Diehl, P. (2009) Peacekeeping and Beyond. in J. Bercovitch, V. Kremenyuk, & I. W. Zartman eds. *The SAGE Handbook of Conflict Resolution*, Sage Publications Ltd., London.

Dolan, P., Canavan, J. & Pinkerton, J. (2006) *Family Support as Reflective Practice*, Jessica Kingsley, London.

Douglas, K. (2004) 'Processes for Dealing with Conflict in the Workplace: Meeting Feminist Concerns Regarding Mediation', in S. Charlesworth & M. Fastenau, eds, *Women and Work*, RMIT, Melbourne, 1: 85–104.

Dominelli, L. (2009) 'Anti-oppressive Practice in Context', in R. Adams, L. Dominelli & M. Payne, eds, *Social Work: Themes, Issues and*

Critical Debates, 3rd ed., Palgrave, London.

Dominelli, L. & McLeod, E. (1989) *Feminist Social Work*, Macmillan Press, London.

Dunn, D. (2004), 'Narrative Mediation and Workplace Conflict', paper presented at the 7th National Mediation Conference, Darwin.

Durch, W., Holt, V., Earle, C. & Shanahan, M. (2003). The Brahimi Report and the Future of UN Peace Operations, The Henry L Simpson Centre, Washington DC.

Ekman, P. Friesen, W., Wallave, V., O'Sullivan, M., Chan, A., Diacoyanni-Tarlatzis, I., Heider, K., Krause, R., Le Compte, W., Pitcairn, T., Ricci-Bitti, P. et al. (1987). 'Universals and Cultural Differences in the Judgments of Facial Expressions of Emotions', *Journal of Personality and Social Psychology*, 53 (4): 712–717.

Edelstein, M. (2004), 'Mediations: A Cautionary Approach', *Law Institute Journal*, August, Law Institute of Victoria, Melbourne, 38–42.

Egan, G. (2006) *Exercises in Helping Skills*, Thompson Brookes/Cole, California.

— (2013) *The Skilled Helper*, 10th ed., Cenage Learning Inc., California.

Elix, J. (2005) *The Meaning of Success – Measuring Outcomes in Public Policy Dispute Resolution*, University of Western Sydney, NSW.

Erikson, E.H. (1980) *Identity and Life Cycle*, W.W. Norton, New York.

Eunson, J. (1997) *Dealing with Conflict*, John Wiley & Sons, Brisbane.

Evans, S. (2005) 'Beyond Gender: Class Poverty and Domestic Violence', *Australian Social Work*, 58 (1).

Fader, J. & Traylor, L. (2015). 'Dealing with Difference in Desistance Theory: The Promise of Intersectionality for New Avenues of Inquiry', *Sociology Compass*, 9 (4): 247–260.

Faulkes, W. (1990) 'The Modern Development of Alternative Dispute Resolution in Australia', *Alternative Dispute Resolution Journal*, 61–8.

Fawcett, B. (2011). 'Post-modernism in Social Work', in V. Cree, ed., *Social Work: A Reader*, Routledge, Abingdon, Oxon, 227–235.

Fawcett, B. & Waugh, F., eds., (2008) *Addressing Violence, Abuse and Oppression: Debates and Challenges*, Routledge, London.

Foucault, M. (1982) 'The Subject and Power', *Critical Inquiry*, 8 (4): 777–795.

Fox, B. (2017). 'It's Nature and Nurture: Integrating Biology and Genetics into the Social Learning Theory of Criminal Behaviour', *Journal of Criminal Justice*, 49: 22–31.

Field, R. (2005) 'Federal Family Law Reform in 2005: The Problems and Pitfalls for Women and Children of an Increased Emphasis on Post-separation Informal Dispute Resolution', *QUT Law and Justice Journal*, 5: 1–26, http://www.law.qut.edu.au/about/ljj/editions/v5n1/ accessed 6 February 2007.

— (2006) 'Using the Feminist Critique of Mediation to Explore the Good, the Bad and the Ugly: Implications for Women of the Introduction of Mandatory Family Dispute Resolution in Australia', *Australian Journal of Family Law*, 20: 45–78.

Fisher R. & Ertel, B. (1995) *Getting Ready to Negotiate: The Getting to Yes Workbook*, Penguin, New York.

Fisher, R. & Ury, W., eds., (1992) *Getting to Yes: Negotiating Agreement Without Giving In*, 2nd ed., Arrow Business Books, London.

Fisher, T. (2006) 'Transformative Mediation: Differentiating principles from Illusions – Part 1', *ADR Bulletin*, 9: 44–47.

Flynn, D. (2005) 'The Social Worker as Family Mediator: Balancing Power in Cases Involving Family Violence', *Australian Social Work*, 58 (4): 407–418.

Fook, J. (2012) *Social Work: A Critical Approach to Practice*, Sage Publications, London.

Forrester, J. (1999) *The Deliberative Practitioner*, MIT Press, London.

Frederico M., Cooper, B. & Picton C. (1998) *Mediation and Cultural Values: A Model of Culturally Sensitive Mediation*, Department of Immigration and Multicultural Affairs, AGPS, Canberra.

Gaynier L. (2005) 'Transformative Mediation: In Search of a Theory of Practice,' *Conflict Resolution Quarterly*, 22: 397–408.

Gale, C. (2006) 'Collaborative Family Law', paper presented at Law Institute of Victoria Small Practice Conference, Saturday 17 June, Melbourne.

Galaway, B. (1988) 'Crime Victim and Offender Mediation as a Social Work Strategy', *Social Services Review*, 62: 668–683.

Gibelman M. & Demone H. (1989) 'The Social Worker as Mediator in the Legal System', *Social Casework: The Journal of Contemporary Social Work*, USA.

Halperin, E. (2014) 'Emotion, Emotion Regulation and Conflict Resolution', *Emotion Review*, 6 (1) : 68–76.

Harinck, F. & Van Kleef, G. (2012) 'Be Hard on the Interests and Soft on the Values: Conflict Issue Moderates the Effect of Anger in Negotiations', *British Journal of Social Psychology*, 51: 741–752.

Hart, E. & van Ginneken, E. (2017) *New Perspectives on Desistance Theoretical and Empirical Developments*, Palgrave MacMillan, London.

Folger, J., Poole, M. & Strutman, R. (2001). *Working Through Conflict: Strategies for Relationships, Groups and Organizations*, Longman, New York.

Giordano, M. & Wolf, A. (2003) 'Sharing Waters: Post Rio international Water Management', *Natural Resources Forum*, 27: 163–171.

Hargreaves Heap, S & Varoufakis, Y. (2004) *Game Theory*, Routledge, London and New York.

Haynes, J. & Charlesworth, S. (1996) *The Fundamentals of Family Mediation*, The Federation Press, NSW.

Healey, K. (1995) *Conflict Resolution: Issues for the Nineties*, Spinney Press, Australia.

Hedberg, J., Charlesworth, S. & Lanteri, A. (1985) 'Learning Clinical Practice by Simulation in Law and Social Work', *Australian Social Work*, 38 (3).

Herrnstein, B. (1996) 'Women and Mediation: A chance to Speak and to be Heard', *Mediation Quarterly*, 3: 229–241.

Hibberd, P. & Newman, P. (1999) *Alternative Dispute Resolution and Adjudication in Construction Disputes*, Blackwell, London.

Hu Min (2013) 'Law for Elderly Creates a Legal Conundrum', *Shanghai Daily*, Monday 8 July, 4.

Ife, J. (1997) *Rethinking Social Work: Towards Critical Practice*, Addison Wesley Longman, Melbourne.

— (2012) *Human Rights and Social Work: Towards Rights Based Practice*, Cambridge University Press, Melbourne.

Infante, D. & Wigley, C. (1986) 'Verbal Aggressiveness: An Interpersonal Mode and Measure', *Communication Monograph*s, 53: 61–69.

Infante, D., Sabourin, T. Rudd, J. & Shannon, E. (1990) 'Verbal Aggression in Violent and Non-violent Martial Disputes', *Communication Quarterly*, 38: 361–367.

Infante, D., Riddle, B., Hovarth, C., and Tumlin, S. (1992) 'Verbal Aggressiveness: Messages and Reasons', *Communication Quarterly*, 42: 72–80.

International Commission of Intervention and State Sovereignty (2001). The Responsibility to Protect: Report of the International Commission of Intervention and State Sovereignty, International Development Research Centre, Otawa, Canada.

Islam, M.S. (2013) *Development, Power and the Environment*, Routledge, New York.

IUCN/UNEP/WWF (1980) World Conservation Strategy, Gland, Switzerland.

Islam, M.S. (2013) *Development, Power and the Environment*, Routledge, New York.

Jameson, J. Bodtker, M. & Linker, T. (2010) 'Facilitating Conflict Transformation: Mediation Strategies for Eliciting Emotional Communication in a Workplace Conflict', *Negotiation Journal*, January, 24–47.

Jeong, H. W. (2010) *Conflict Management and Resolution: An Introduction*, Routledge, London.

High Level Independent Panel on United Nations Peace Operations (2015). Uniting Our Strengths for Peace: Politics, Partnership and People: Report of the High Level Independent Panel on United Nations Peace Operations, United Nations, Washington DC.

Johnson, D. (2014) *Reaching Out: Interpersonal Effectiveness and Self-Actualisation*, 11th ed., Pearson, Boston.

Jordan, P. Troth, A. (2004) 'Managing Emotions During Team Problem Solving: Emotional Intelligence and Conflict Resolution', *Human Performance*, 17 (2): 195–218.

Kaldor, M. (2012) *New and Old Wars: Organised Violence in a Global Era*. Polity Press, Oxford.

Kanske, P. & Kotz, S. (2011a) 'Emotion Speeds up Conflict Resolution: A New Role for theVentral Anterior Cingulate Cortex', *Cerebral Cortex*, 21: 911–919.

Kanske, P. & Kotz, S. (2011b) 'Emotion Triggers Executive Attention: Anterior Cingulate Cortex and Amygdala Responses to Emotional Words in a Conflict Task', *Human Brain Mapping*, 32: 198–208.

Karyabwite, D.R. (2000) Water Sharing in the Nile River Valley http://www.grid.unep.ch/activities/sustainable/nile/nilereport.pdf accessed 23 January 2005.

Kennedy, K., Simonovic, S., Tejada-Guibert, A., Doria, M. & Martin, J. (2009) *IWRM Implementation in Basins, Sub-basins and Aquifers*, International Hydrological Programme of UNESCO, Paris.

Keobang, A. Keola (2002) 'National Report on the Prevention and Resolution of Environmental Conflicts in the Mekong River Basin (LAOPDR), STEA', paper presented at MRC regional workshop on Con-flict Resolution in the Mekong River Basin, Phnom Penh.

Kolb, D. (1984) *Experiential Learning: Experience as the Source of Learning and Development*, Prentice Hall, New Jersey.

Kraybill, S.R., Evans, R.A. & Evans, A.F. (2001) *Peace Skills – Manual for Community Mediators*, Jossey-Bass Inc., California.

Kress, G., ed. (1996) *Communication and Culture: An Introduction*, New South Wales University Press, Kensington.

Lang, W., ed. (1995) *Sustainable Development and International Law*, Graham and Trotman, London.

Laohasiriwong, S. (2002) 'National Report on the Prevention and Resolution of Environmental Conflicts in the Mekong River Basin, (Thailand)', paper presented at MRC regional workshop, Phnom Penh.

Lazarus, R. (1991) *Emotion and Adaptation*, Oxford University Press, New York.

Leigey, M. (2019) 'Female Institutional Misconduct: A Test of Deprivation, Importation, and Gendered Importation Theories', *The Prison Journal*, 99 (3): 343–362.

Luckin, D & Sharpe, L. (2005) 'Exploring the community waste sector, Are sustainable development and social capital useful concepts for project-level research?', *Community Development Journal*, 40 (1): 62–75.

Lund, M. (2012) 'Conflict Prevention: Theory in Pursuit of Policy and

Practice', in J. Bercovitch, V. Kremenyuk, & I. W. Zartman (eds) *The SAGE Handbook of Conflict Resolution*, Sage Publications Ltd., London.

Mack, K. (2003) *Court Referral to ADR: Criteria and Research*, National Alternative Dispute Resolution Advisory Council and Australian Institute of Judicial Administration, Canberra.

Magga, G. (2010) 'Uganda: Ethiopian Led River Nile Agreement Signed Without Egypt and Sudan', *Afrik News*, Friday 14 May.

Maida, P. (1995) 'Mediating Environmental Disputes: Borrowing Ideas from a Law and Economics Perspectiv', in J. Blackburn & W. Bruce (1995).

Martin, J. (2000) 'Social Workers as Mediators', *Australian Social Work*, 43 (4): 33–39.

— (2003) 'Historical Development of Critical Social Work Practice', in J. Allan, B. Pease & L. Briskman, *Critical Social Work: An Introduction to Theories and Practices*, Allen & Unwin, NSW.

— (2012) *Mental Health Social Work*, Ginninderra Press, Port Adelaide.

Martin, J. & Buxton, M. (2007) 'Socio-economic and Ecological Issues in the Mekong River Basin', *The International Journal of Interdisciplinary Social Sciences*, 2 (4): 251–259.

Martin, J., Buxton, M. & Kelly, M.

(2006) 'Policy Making Mediation in the Mekong River Basin', *Just Policy*, 41: 26–32.

Martin, J. & Douglas, K. (2007) 'Family Dispute Resolution: Social Work Theory and Practice Considerations', *Australian Social Work*, 60 (3): 295–307.

Martin, J. (2015). 'A Strengths Approach to Elder Mediation', *Conflict Resolution Quarterly*, 32, 481–98.

Maidment, J. & Egan, R. (2009) *Practice Skills in Social Work and Welfare: More Than Just Common Sense*, 2nd ed. Allen and Unwin, NSW.

Maslow, A. (1998) *Toward a Psychology of Being*, 3rd ed., John Wiley & Sons, New York.

Mather, M., Lighthall, N., Nga, L. & Gorlick, M. (2010) 'Sex Differences in How Stress Affects Brain Activity During Face Viewing', *Neuroreport*, 21 (14): 933–7.

Mayer, B. (2004) *Beyond Neutrality*, Jossey-Bass, San Francisco.

Mayer, J. & Salovey, P. (1997) 'What is Emotional Intelligence?' in P. Salovey and D. Sluyter eds. *Emotional Development and Emotional Intelligence: Implications for Educators*, Basic Books, New York.

McCaffery, S. (2000) 'Water, Water Everywhere, but Too Few Drops to Drink: The Coming Fresh Water Crisis and International Environmental Law', *Denver Journal of International Law and Policy*, 28 (3): 325.

McIntosh, J., Long, M & Wells, Y. (2009) *Children Beyond Dispute*, Attorney General's Department, Canberra.

Mediation Association of Victoria (1997) *ADR Directory*, Mediation Association of Victoria, Melbourne.

Mekong River Commission (2000) Long Term Environment Program 2001–2005, MRC, Phnom Penh.

— (2001) MRC Hydropower Development Strategy, MRC, Phnom Penh.

— (2002) Basin Development Plan Inception Report, MRC, Phnom Penh.

— (2002) Mekong River Basin Guidelines for Experts, Phnom Penh, Cambodia.

Minichiello, V., Aroni, R., Timewell E. & Alexander L. (1995) *In-depth Interviewing*, 2nd ed., Longman, Melbourne.

Minnery, J.R. (1985) *Conflict Management in Urban Planning*, Gower, London.

Minuchin, S. (1974) *Families and Family Therapy*, Harvard University Press, Cambridge.

Mohan,T., McGregor, H. & Stranzo, Z. (1992) *Communicating: Theory and Practice*, 3rd ed., Harcourt Brace Jovanovich, Sydney.

Molan, L. (1999) *Children's Voices in Family Mediation*, Graduate School of Education, LaTrobe University, Bundoora.

Moloney, L. (2005) 'Government's Response to the Family Law Maze: the Family Relationship Centres Proposal', *Journal of Family Studies* 11 (1): 11–35.

Moreau, M.J. (1977) A Structural Approach to Social Work, unpublished paper, Carleton University School of Social Work, Ontario.

— (1979) 'A Structural Approach to Social Work Practice', *Canadian Journal of Social Work Education*, 5(1): 78–94.

Movius, K. & Susskind, L. (2009) *Built to Win: Creating a World Class Negotiating Organization*, Harvard Business Press, New York.

Mullaly, B. (2006) *The New Structural Social Work: Ideology, Theory and Practice*, Oxford University Press, UK.

National Alternative Dispute Resolution Advisory Council (NADRAC) (1997) Primary Dispute Resolution in Family Law: A Report to the Attorney-General on Part 5 of the Family Law Regulations, Commonwealth of Australia, Canberra.

— (2000) The Development of Standards for ADR Discussion Paper, Commonwealth of Australia, Canberra.

— (2001) A Framework for ADR Standards, Commonwealth of Australia, Canberra.

— (2002) Development of Standards for ADR: Report, Commonwealth of Australia, Canberra.

— (2004) Who Says You're a Mediator: Towards a National System for Accrediting Mediators, Commonwealth of Australia, Canberra.

— (2012) Your Guide to Dispute

Resolution, Commonwealth of Australia, Canberra.

Native Title Research Unit (1998) Working with the Native Title Act: Alternatives to the Adversarial Method, Australian Institute of Aboriginal and Torres Strait Islander Studies, Canberra.

Nebel, B. & Wright, R. (1999) *Environmental Science: The Way the World Works*, 7th ed., Prentice-Hall, New Jersey.

Neilson, L. (1994) 'Mediators and Lawyers: Perception of Education and Training in Family Mediation', *Mediation Quarterly*, 12 (2).

Neisser, U., (1982) *Memory Observed: Remembering in Natural Contexts*, W.H. Freeman & Co., San Francisco.

Neou, Bonheur, (1992) National Report on the Prevention and Resolution of Environmental Conflicts in the Lower Mekong River Basin (Cambodia), paper presented at MRC regional workshop on Conflict Resolution in the Mekong River Basin, Cambodian Ministry of Environment, Phnom Penh.

Nile Basin Initiative (2005) Sequence of Major Events of the Nile Basin Initiative Process, Nile Basin Initiative Secretariat,http://www.nilebasin.org/nbihistory.htm, accessed 23 January 2005.

O'Connell, T. & Moore, D. (1994) *Wagga Juvenile Cautioning Process: The General Applicability of Family Group Conferences for Juvenile Offenders and their Victims*, Rural Society, Wagga Wagga.

O'Connor, I., Wilson J. & Setterlund D. (2003) *Social Work and Welfare Practice*, 3rd ed., Pearson Education, Melbourne.

Olson, L. & Braithwaite, D. (2004) 'If You Hit Me Again, I'll Hit You Back: Conflict Management Strategies of Individuals Experiencing Aggression During Conflicts', *Communication Studies*, 55 (2): 271–285.

Orme, J. (2009) 'Feminist Social Work', in R. Adams, L. Dominelli, & M. Payne, eds, *Social Work: Themes, Issues and Critical Debates*, Macmillan, London, 218–228.

Ozanne, E. (1998) 'Social Assessment and the Elderly', in R.W. Warne & D.N. Prinsley, *A Manual of Geriatric Care*, Williams & Wilkins, NSW.

Parsons, R. (1991) 'The Mediator Role in Social Work', *Social Work*, 36 (6).

Payne, M. (2005) *Modern Social Work Theory*, 3rd ed., Palgrave, London.

Pessoa, L. (2009) 'How do Emotions and Motivation Direct Executive Control?', *Trends in Cognitive Sciences*, 13 (4): 160–6.

Phillips, J. (1997) 'The Future of Social Work with Older People in a Changing World', in N. Parton, *Social Theory, Social Change and Social Work*, Routledge, UK.

Phung, Chi Sy, (2002) National Report on the Prevention and Resolution of Environmental Conflicts in the Mekong River Basin - Vietnam, NEA, paper presented at MRC regional workshop on Conflict Resolution in the Mekong River Basin, Phnom Penh.

Pines, A., Gat, H. & Tal, Y. (2002) 'Gender Differences in Content and Style of Argument Between Couples During Divorce Mediation', *Conflict Resolution Quarterly*, 20: 23–50.

Planning Reform Unit (1997) *How to Get the Best Out of Planning: A Guide to Facilitating Meetings*, Victorian Government, Melbourne.

Ralph, S., (1997) 'Working with Aboriginal Families', *Family Matters*, No. 46, Autumn, Australian Institute of Family Studies, Melbourne.

Ramsbotham, O., Miall, H., & Woodhouse, T. (2011) *Contemporary Conflict Resolution*, Polity Press, Cambridge.

Regan, S. (1998) Everything You Wanted to Know About Family Mediation in New South Wales but Were Afraid to Ask: A Survey of Family Mediation in NSW, paper presented at Family Mediation Seminar, 28 May 1998, Surrey Hills, NSW.

Retzinger, S. & Scheff, T. (2000) 'Emotion, Alienation and Narratives: Resolving Intractable Conflict', *Mediation Quarterly*, 18: 71–85.

Rhoades, H., Astor, H., Sanson, A. & O'Connor, M. (2008) *Enhancing Inter-professional Relationships in a Changing Family Law System*, University of Melbourne, Melbourne.

Ricci I. (2012) *Mum's House, Dad's House*, Fireside, New York.

Rispens, R. & Demerouti, E. (2016). 'Conflict at Work, Negative Emotions and Performance: A Diary Study', *Negotiation and Conflict Management Research*, 9 (2): 103–119.

Roediger, H., Neisser, U. & Winograd, E. (1990). 'Remembering Reconsidered: Ecological and Traditional Approaches to the Study of Memory', *The American Journal of Psychology*, 103 (3): 403–9.

Rocque, M. (2017). *Desistance from Crime: New Advances in Theory and Research*, Palgrave Macmillan, New York.

Rogan, R. & La France, B. (2003) 'An Examination of the relationship Between Verbal Aggressiveness, Conflict Management Strategies and Conflict Interaction Goals', *Communication Quarterly*, 51 (4): 458–469.

Roediger, H., Neisser, U. & Winograd, E. (1990). 'Remembering Reconsidered: Ecological and Traditional Approaches to the Study of Memory', *The American Journal of Psychology*, 103 (3): 403–9.

Saposnek, D. (1998) *Mediating Child Custody Disputes*, Jossey-Bass, San Francisco.

Scheff, T.J. (1968) 'Negotiating Reality: Notes on Power in the Assessment of Responsibility', *Social Problems*, 16 (1): 3–7.

Scott, M. (2004) 'Collaborative Law: A New Role for Lawyers', *Aus-*

tralasian Dispute Resolution Journal, 15: 207–216.

Severson, M. & Bankston, T. (1995) 'Social Work and the Pursuit of Justice Through Mediation', Social Work, 40 (5).

Shailor, J. (1994) Empowerment in Dispute Resolution: A Critical Analysis of Communication, Praeger, London.

Shanghai Daily (2013) 'Thirty-Six Stratagems: Ancient Ruses Can Still Be Useful', Ancient Wisdom, Shanghai Daily, 7 July.

Sheehan, R. (2006) 'Alternative Dispute Resolution in Child Protection Matters', Australian Social Work, 59 (2): 157–171.

Sillars, A. (1985) 'Interpersonal Perception in Relationships', Chapter 12 in W. Ickes ed. Compatible and Incompatible Relationships, Springer-Verlag, New York.

Singer, L. (1994) Settling Disputes: Conflict Resolution in Business, Families and the Legal System, 2nd ed., Westview Press, Colorado.

Slotboom, A., Kruttschnitt, C., Bijleveld, C. & Menting, B. (2011) 'Psychological Wellbeing of Incarcerated Women in The Netherlands: Importation or Deprivation', Punishment and Society, 13 (2): 176–197.

Smith, H. & Pettigrew, T. (2015) 'Advances in Relative Deprivation Theory and Research', Social Justice Research, 28 (1): 1–6.

Smyth, B. & Moloney, L. (2003) 'Therapeutic Divorce Mediation: Strengths, Limitations and Future

Directions', Journal of Family Studies, 9: 161–186.

Sourdin, T. (2012) Alternative Dispute Resolution, 4th ed., Lawbook, Sydney.

Sourdin, T, Fisher, T. & Moloney, M. (2004) Towards Quality Standards for Family Dispute Practitioners: Research Report, La Trobe University, Bundoora.

Sourdin, T. & Balvin, N. (2009) 'Mediation in the Supreme and County Courts of Victoria: ASummary of the Results', ADR Bulletin, 11 (3), Article 1:1.

Spegel, N., Rogers, B. & Buckley, R. (1998) Negotiation, Butterworths, Australia.

Staughton D. (2006) How to Find and Keep the Best Staff, paper presented at the Small Practice Conference, Law Institute of Victoria, Melbourne.

Susskind, L. (1999a) Better Environmental Studies, Island Press, New York.

— (1999b) Negotiating Environmental Agreements, Island Press, New York.

— (1999c) Using Assisted Negotiation to Settle Land Use Disputes, The Consensus Building Institute and The Lincoln Institute of Land Policy, New York.

— (2000a) The Consensus Building Handbook, Sage, Mew York.

— (2000b) Mediating Land Use Disputes, Pros and Cons, Lincoln Institute of Land Policy, New York.

Susskind, L. & Crump, L. (2008) *Multiparty Negotiation*, Sage, New York.

Susskind, L. & Field P. (1996) *Dealing with an Angry Public: the Mutual Gains Approach to Resolving Conflict*, The Free Press, New York.

Susskind, L. & Saleem, H. (2014) *Environmental Diplomacy: Negotiating Effective International Agreements*, 2nd ed., Oxford University Press, London.

Swain, A. (2001) 'Water Wars: Fact or Fiction', *Futures*, October–November, 769–776.

Swain, P. & Ban, P. (1997) 'Participation and Partnership: Family Group Conferencing in the Australian Context', *Journal of Social Welfare and Family Law*, 19 (1): 35–42.

Tanaka, A., Raishevich, N. & Scarpa, A. (2010) 'Family Conflict and Childhood Aggression: The Role of Child Anxiety', *Journal of Interpersonal Violence*, 25 (1): 2127–2143.

Taylor, A. (2002) *The Handbook of Family Dispute Resolution: Theory and Practice*, Wiley Bass, USA.

Tesoriero, M. (2006) 'Reasonable Fear of Violence', *Law Institute Journal*, 80: 81.

Thompson, N. (1998) *Promoting Equality: Challenging Discrimination and Oppression in the Human Services*, Macmillan, London.

Tillet, G. & French, B. (2006) *Resolving Conflict: A Practical Approach*, Oxford University Press, Melbourne.

Tipler, J. (2000) *Successful Negotiating*, Marshall Publishing, London.

Todorski, J. (1995) 'Attachment and Divorce: A Therapeutic View', *Journal of Divorce and Remarriage*, 22 (3).

Tow, D. & Stubbs, M. (1997) 'The Effectiveness of Alternative Dispute Resolution Methods in Planning Disputes', *Australian Dispute Resolution Journal*, February, 267–81.

Toyne, P. (1995) *The Reluctant Nation*, ABC Books, Sydney.

Ting-Toomey, S. (1994). *The Challenge of Facework*, State University of New York Press, Albany, New York.

Umbreit, M. (1991) 'Mediation of Youth Conflict: A Multi-System Perspective', *Child and Adolescent Social Work*, 18 (2l).

UNDP (2001) Nile Basin Initiative, UNDP Sustainable Water Management, available at http://www.undp .org/seed/water/region/nile.htm accessed 7 October 2002.

United Nations (1993) *International Environmental Law: Emerging Trends and Implications for Transnational Companies*, Department of Economic and Social Development, Transnational Corporations and Management Division, New York.

United Nations (2015) Performance Peacekeeping: Final Report of the Expert Panel on Technology and Innovation in UN Peacekeeping, The United Nations, Washington DC.

Victorian Law Reform Commission (2006) Review of Family Violence Laws: Report, Melbourne.

ViTrade (1999) 'Sudan Warns Nile Basin Partners Against Foreign Interference: ViTrade Global Financial Risk Analysis, http://.vitrade.com/sudan accessed 7 October 2002.

Verwey, W. (1992) 'Opening Speech', in Bilderbeek, S., ed., *Biodiversity and International Law*, Netherlands National Committee for the International Union for Conservation of Nature and Natural Resources, IOS Press, Amsterdam.

Wallensteen, P. (2019) *Understanding Conflict Resolution*. Sage Publications Ltd., London.

Walters, G. & Crawford, G. (2013) 'In and Out of Prison: Do Importation Factors Predict All Forms of Misconduct or Just the More Serious Ones?', *Journal of Criminal Justice*, 41 (6): 407–413.

Ward, J. & Brown, C. (2015) *Social Learning Theory and Crime*, Elsevier Ltd., Florida, USA.

Wearing, B. (1986) 'Feminist Theory in Social Work', in H. Marchant & B. Wearing, eds., *Gender Reclaimed: Women in Social Work*, Hale & Iremonger, NSW.

Webb, T. (2017) 'Men, Masculinities and Violence', New Community, 14 (4): 23–33.

White, M. (1997) *Let's Be Reasonable: A Guide to Resolving Disputes*, Choice Books, NSW.

White, R. & Graham, H. (2010) *Working with Offenders: A Guide to Concepts and Practices*, William Publishing, New York.

Windslade, J. & Monk, G. (2001) *Narrative Mediation*, Jossey-Bass, San Francisco.

Wolf, A.T., Stahl, K. & Macomber, M. (2003) 'Conflict and Co-operation Within International River Basins: The Importance of Institutional Capacity', *Water Resources Update*, Vol. 125, Universities Council on Water Resources.

World Commission on Dams (2000) *Dams and Development: A New Framework for Decision-Making*, Earthscan, London.

World Commission on Environment and Development (1987) *Our Common Future*, Oxford University Press, Oxford.

Worldwide Fund for Nature (2002) *Managing Water Wisely: Promoting Sustainable Development Through Integrated River Basin Management*, WWF-UK, Surrey.

Zhanh, Q., Ting-Toomey, S. & Oetzal, J. (2014). 'Linking Emotion to the Conflict Face-Negotiation Theory: A U/S.-China Investigation of the mediating Effects of Anger, Compassion, and Guilt in Interpersonal Conflict' *Human Communication Research*, 40: 373–395.

Zhao Wen (2013) 'Taobao Offers Option to Hire Someone to Visit Parents', *Shanghai Daily*, Monday 8 July, 4.

Notes

1

1. K. Clements & R. Ward (1994).

2. Conflict Resolution Network (1993).

3. S. Retzinger & T. Scheff (2000).

4. K. Cloke & J. Goldsmith (2007).

5. J. Jameson, M. Bodtker & T. Linker (2010).

6. R.B. Bush & J. Folger (2005).

7. R. Rispens & E. Demerouti (2016).

8. T. Webb (2017).

9. Q. Zhang, S. Ting-Toomey & J. Oetzal (2014).

10. E. Halperin (2014).

11. P. Ekman et al. (1987).

12. L. Olson & D. Braithwaite (2004).

13. Q. Zhang, S. Ting-Toomey & J. Oetzal (2014).

14. R. Rogan & B. La France (2003).

15. S. Ting-Toomey (1994).

16. Q. Zhang, S. Ting-Toomey & J. Oetzal (2014).

17. Q. Zhang, S. Ting-Toomey & J. Oetzal (2014).

18. J. Jameson, M. Bodtker & T. Linker (2010).

19. L. Pessoa (2009).

20. P. Kanske & S. Koz (2011a).

21. P. Kanske & S. Koz (2011b).

22. R. Arbel, A. Rodriguez & G. Margolin (2016).

23. L. Aloia & D. Solomon (2015).

24. A. Tanaka, N. Raishevich & A. Scarpa (2010).

25. R. Arbel, A. Rodriguez & G. Margolin (2016).

26. M. Mather, N. Lighthall, L. Nga & M. Gorlick (2010).

27. L. Bloomer et al. (2014).

28. R. Lazarus (1991).

29. J. Jameson, M. Bodtker & T. Linker (2010).

30. A. Sillars (1985).

31. J. Mayer & P. Salovey (1997).

32. T. Jordan & A. Troth (2004).

33. J. Jameson, M. Bodtker & T. Linker (2010).

34. J. Jameson, M. Bodtker & T. Linker (2010).

35. L. Aloia & D. Solomon (2015).

36. R. Rispens & E. Demerouti (2016).

37. R. Rispens & E. Demerouti (2016).

38. T. Jordan & A. Troth (2004).

39. F. Harinck & G. Van Kleef (2003).

40. A.Tanaka, N. Raishevich & A. Scarpa (2010).

41. L. Olson & D. Braithwaite (2004).

42. T. Webb (2017).

43. T. Webb (2017).

44. T. Webb (2017).

45. D. Infante & C. Wigley (1986).

46. D. Infante, B. Riddle, C. Hovarth, & Tumlin, S. (1992).

47. R. Rogan & B. La France (2003).

48. R. Rogan & B. La France (2003).

49. T. Webb (2017).

50. J. Jameson, M. Bodtker & T. Linker (2010).

51. L. Olson & D. Braithwaite (2004).

52. D. Infante, T. Sabourin, J. Rudd, J. & E. Shannon (1990).

53. J. Folger, M. Poole & R. Strutman (2001).

54. N. Brill (1995).

55. N. Brill (1995).

56. G. Kress (1996).

57. M. Frederico, B. Cooper & C. Picton (1998).

58. J. Martin (2000).

2

1. Conflict Resolution Network (1993).

2. S. Kraybill, R, Evans & A. Evans (2001).

3. Conflict Resolution Network (1993).

4. R. Dreikurs (1964).

5. Issues of violence are discussed further in chapters 4 and 8.

3

1. NADRAC (2012).

2. L. Boulle (2011).

3. AIMA (2013), l.

4. NADRAC (2012), 13.

5. NADRAC (2012), 13.

6. B. Smythe & L. Moloney (2003).

7. L. Boulle (2011).

8. L. Boulle (2011).

9. L. Boulle (2011).

10. D. Dunn (2004).

11. L. Susskind (2014).

12. D. Della Noce (1999).

13. Conflict Resolution Network (1993).

14. NADRAC (2012), 13.

15. R. Fisher & W. Ury (1992).

16. P. Adler (1998).

17. NADRAC (2001).

4

1. L. Boulle (2011), 1.

2. Attorney General's Department (1996), 131.

3. M. Payne (2005).

4. S.Y. Hargreaves, Heap & Varoufakis (2004).

5. *Shanghai Daily* (2013).

6. Anon. (2014).

7. M. Moreau (1979).

8. M. Moreau (1979).

9. L. Dominelli & E. McLeod (1989), 173.

10. B. Burke & P. Harrison (1998)

11. L. Dominelli (2009).

12. L. Dominelli (2009).

13. N. Thompson (1998).

14. J. Dalrymple & B.Burke (2006).

15. M. Foucault (1982).

16. M. Roque (2017).

17. E. Hart & E. van Ginneken (2017).

18. S.Y. Fader & J.L. Traylor (2015).

19. R. White & H. Graham (2010).

20. J. Ward & C. Brown (2015).

21. R. White & H. Graham (2010).

22. R. Akers (2017).

23. B. Fox (2017).

24. H. Smith & T. Pettigrew (2015).

25. B. Burraston, J. McCutcheon & S. Watts (2018).

26. Slotboom, Kruttschnitt, Bijleveld & Menting (2011).

27. Choi & Dulisse, (2020).

28. Walters & Crawford (2013).

29. M. Leigey (2019).

30. See chapter 7 for a postmodern critique of ageing.

31. J. Haley (1971).

32. See S. Minuchin (1974).

33. M. Bogo & E. Vayda (1987).

34. J. Martin, E. McKay & L. Hawkins (2006).

35. J. Fook (2012).

5

1. L. Boulle and M. Nesci (2001).

2. L. Susskind (20 14).

3. S. Charlesworth & J. Haynes (1996).

4. H. Astor (2000).

5. D. Flynn (2005).

6. J. Maidment & R. Egan (2009).

7. J. Martin (2012).

8. S. Cobb (1993).

9. S. Cobb & J. Rifkin (1991).

10. J. Fook (2012).

11. G. Egan (2013).

6

1. Conflict Resolution Network (1993).

2. Conflict Resolution Network (1993).

3. I. Ricci 1 (997).

4. L. Susskind (2014).

5. P. Adler (1998).

7

1. J. Martin (2001).

2. Native Title Research Unit (1998).

3. L. Boulle (20011).

4. Mediation Association of Victoria (1997).

5. W. Faulkes (1990).

6. Mediation Association of Victoria (1997).

7. NADRAC (2004).

8. R. Field (2006).

9. J.Martin & K. Douglas (2007).

10. Astor & Chinkin (2002); Flyn (2005).

11. Astor & Chinkin (2002).

12. Refer to the discussion of types of relationships in Chapter 6.

13. C. Gale (2006), 1.

14. See chapter 4 for a discussion of the mutual gains approach.

15. M. Umbreit (1991).

16. S. Regan (1998).

17. J. Martin (2015).

18. HuMin (2013), 4.

19. Zhao Wen (2013), 4.

20. See chapter 4 for details of life cycle and postmodem theories.

21. B. Fawcett (2011).

22. E. Ozanne (1998).

23. D. Dunn (2004).

24. K. Douglas (2004).

25. See the discussion of critical theory in chapter 4.

26. N. Christie (1977).

27. B. Galaway (1988).

28. P. Swain.& P. Ban (1997).

29. Braithwaite & Strang (2016).

30. T. O'Connell & D. Moore (1994).

31. Christie (1977).

32. White & Graham (2010).

33. NADRAC (2012).

34. J. Forrester (1999).

35. Planning Reform Unit (1997).

36. Planning Institute of Australia (2006).

37. J. Minnery (1985).

38. D. Tow & M. Stubbs (1997).

8

1. M. Buxton, J. Martin & M. Kelly (2006).

2. L. Susskind (2014).

3. J. Elix (2005), 2.

4. J. Elix (2005).

5. P. Toyne (1995), 2.

6. IUCN/UNEP/WWF (1980); World Commission on Environment and Development (1987).

7. S. Beder (1993).

8. B. Nebel & R. Wright (1999), 14.

9. K. Clements & R. Ward (1994).

10. This chapter includes extracts from M. Buxton, J. Martin & M. Kelly (2006).

11. S. Laohasiriwong (2002).

12. Mekong River Commission (2000).

13. World Commission on Dams (2000).

14. World Commission on Dams (2000).

15. WWF (2002).

16. A. Swain (2001).

17. D. Karyabwite (2000).

18. D. Karyabwite (2000).

19. A. Swain (2001).

20. J. Dawoud (2001).

21. UNDP (2001), 10.

22. Nile Basin Initiative (2005).

23. Nile Basin Initiative (2005).

24. M. Buxton (2003).

25. Quoted in ViTrade (1999), l.

26. G. Magga (2010), l.

27. M. Buxton (2003).

28. M Giordano & A. Wolf (2003)

29. M. Buxton (2003).

30. M. Buxton (2003).

31. Blomquist et al. (2005).

32. M. Buxton (2003).

33. L. Caflisch (1998).

34. S. McCaffery (2000).

35. W. Lang (1995).

36. M. Buxton (2003).

37. Mekong River Commission (2000).

38. Mekong River Commission (2000).

39. Mekong River Commission (2001), 6.

40. Mekong River Commission (2002).

41. M. Buxton (2003), l32.

42. M.Buxton (2003).

43. Mekong River Commission (2003), l.

44. N. Bonheur (2002).

45. N. Bonheur (2002).

46. S. Laohasiriwong (2002).

47. *Bangkok Post* (2002).

48. S. Laohasiriwong (2002).

49. S. Laohasiriwong (2002).

50. K. Keloa (2002), 15.

51. N. Bonheur (2002), 2.

52. N. Bonheur (2002), 29.

9

1. P. Wallensteen (2019).

2. M. Kaldor (2012).

3. H.W. Jeong (2010).

4. C. Cunneen, B. Goldson & S. Russell (2016); O. Ramsbotham, H. Miall & T. Woodhouse (2011).

5. C. Cunneen, B. Goldson & S. Russell (2016); O. Ramsbotham, H. Miall & T. Woodhouse (2011).

6. O. Ramsbotham, H. Miall & T. Woodhouse (2011).

7. K. Boulding (1999).

8. P. Diehl (2009).

9. M. Lund (2012).

10. P. Diehl (2009).

11. P. Diehl (2009).

12. International Commission of Intervention and State Sovereignty (2001).

13. H.W. Jeong (2010).

14. H.W. Jeong (2010).

15. B. Boutros Ghali (1992).

16. W. Durch, V. Holt, C. Earle & M. Shanahan (2003).

17. HIPPO (2015).

18. United Nations (2015).

www.ingramcontent.com/pod-product-compliance
Lightning Source LLC
Chambersburg PA
CBHW030242030426
42336CB00009B/214